—FEEDING—
The Simple Solution

Beatrice Hollyer
and
Lucy Smith

WARD LOCK

A WARD LOCK BOOK

First published in the UK 1997
by Ward Lock
Wellington House
125 Strand
LONDON
WC2R 0BB

A Cassell Imprint

Distributed in the United States
by Sterling Publishing Co., Inc.
387 Park Avenue South, New York, NY 10016-8810

A British Library Cataloguing in Publication Data block for this book
may be obtained from the British Library

ISBN 0 7063 7645 5

Designed by Chris Warner

Printed and bound in Great Britain by Mackays of Chatham

Cover picture: Collections Sandra Lousada

CONTENTS

FOREWORD

EATING and sleeping are the physical foundations of infancy. If they go smoothly, so does everything else. A baby who sleeps all night and wakes eager for breakfast is easier and happier than one who feeds several times a night and then crossly rejects her meals. Whether your baby is one or the other is no accident of luck.

In our first book, *Sleep: The Secret of Problem-free Nights* (Ward Lock, 1996), Lucy Smith and I described how to read your baby's signals and follow her cues to make sure she sleeps through the night as easily, and as early, as possible. In this book, we apply the same approach to problem-free feeding.

In its simplest form, we need to sleep when tired and to eat when hungry. But that natural balance is easily thrown off course. Feelings run high around both sleep and feeding, precisely because they are so essential to life, and life with small children in particular. Inevitably, they are the first place where conflict shows up. When that happens, problems are the result.

The way to avoid a feeding problem is to make sure that one never develops in the first place. This is much easier than you might imagine. Your child's eating habits are powerfully influenced by her early experience of feeding. With clear, practical information about how she learns to feed, and how her feelings about food are formed, you can make a tremendous difference to how feeding goes for both of you.

Easy feeding in infancy makes for easy feeding throughout childhood. Getting off on the wrong foot, however, can make life difficult from the start. Your baby's ideas are shaped by her early experience, but they quickly develop into firm opinions of her own, as every mother of a toddler knows. If feeding is simple and straightforward from the start, conflict over food can be avoided altogether.

This doesn't mean spending time producing special meals for

7

babies and children. Quite the opposite. The simple solution rests on one central idea:

> *You can feed your baby a nutritious and healthy diet from infancy throughout childhood, while keeping effort, stress, time and expense to a minimum.*

When Lucy and I first talked about a book that would make it easy to avoid feeding problems, we agreed that the key is to keep it simple, but that this isn't always easy. Lucy's experience as a nurse, midwife and health visitor convinced her that a book to simplify the whole business of feeding was even more urgently needed than one on sleep. 'A baby who doesn't sleep can make parents desperate,' says Lucy, 'but food makes people angry.'

The title of this book reflects its central idea: there is a simple, easy way to success without strain or suffering. The key is watching and listening to your baby, interpreting her signals, and responding appropriately. You provide the food, create the setting, set the boundaries and offer help. The rest is up to her.

In this way, eating, like sleeping, gradually becomes something your baby can manage for herself. Part of your job is to trust her to do that. To be able to trust her, you need confidence. Confidence grows when you know what you're doing, and that knowledge is rooted in useful, practical information.

Studying nutritional tables, buying special products, spending ages cooking delicious food which your child refuses to eat – all this is common among parents doing their best to feed their children well. None of it is necessary. The more you worry over your child's eating, the more difficult it is for her to relax and eat in a way that meets her own needs.

This book shows how easy it is to feed your child in a way that lets her learn to eat well for herself. This will guide her into good eating habits that will last her a lifetime, and even help her to feed her own children without fuss.

* * *

The book has been written for the parents and carers of healthy babies. A baby with physical problems needs specialized medical care and feeding advice appropriate to her condition, and that is beyond the scope of this book. However, a baby who has had a difficult start (for example, being born prematurely) will benefit from the simple approach to feeding as soon as she is ready to feed normally.

Ideally, this book should first be read during pregnancy. That is the time to start thinking about how to feed your baby in a way that will avoid problems from the start. New ideas and information acquired then will be in daily use throughout childhood, and make your life as a parent infinitely easier.

The emphasis of the book is on the first year of life, although it's designed to be used from pregnancy throughout childhood. Too often, feeding advice is broken down into narrow age bands, as if the baby was a completely different person from one stage to the next, and from the child she will become. Naturally, her feeding needs change as she progresses from milk-feeding to solids and eventually on to a full mixed diet. But she's also a person from the day she's born, with feelings, character traits and inclinations, all of which make a difference to her eating habits.

Toddlerhood, the age when most feeding conflicts start to make themselves felt, is when attitudes and impressions formed in babyhood will be forcefully expressed. How a baby takes to solids is affected by her early feeding experience. How easily and successfully she moves from first tasting solid food to a full mixed diet has a lot to do with how she learns to eat. A key to the simple solution is treating your baby as a person from the start, with her own needs that should be understood and respected, just as she will gradually learn to understand and respect yours.

For this reason, unless something is clearly intended for a baby or toddler, you will often find the terms 'baby or child', or simply 'child', used when what's being said is relevant to babies, toddlers and children. This is simply to avoid having to repeat 'baby, toddler or child' on every occasion.

Parents of young babies will find several chapters especially for them, but much, especially the chapters on baby food, meals, snacks, drinks and treats, and how conflict over food develops, will be valuable to parents of toddlers and small children as well.

Mothers are often specifically mentioned, naturally in relation to breast-feeding, but also in connection with conflict over food. Partly because of women's historical role as the feeders of their families, it tends to be mothers who mostly handle feeding and the problems that grow up around it. Generally, the book is aimed at either parent or both.

Warm thanks and appreciation are due to the many families who generously shared their experiences (and their mealtimes) with me, and to the countless parents, babies and children with whom Lucy has worked over her fifteen years as a nurse, midwife, health visitor and homeopath. Their discoveries have contributed greatly to this book.

Beatrice Hollyer
London, 1997

NOTE   The question of whether to refer to babies and children as boys or girls is resolved by alternating the terms in successive chapters. So, while in this Foreword 'your baby' is referred to as 'she', in the Introduction which follows 'he' is used, and so on. It seems no worse than other methods and has the advantage of being even-handed.

INTRODUCTION

FEEDING a baby should be the simplest thing. You want to feed him, and he wants to eat. In his first year, when he grows almost as fast as he did in the womb, eating is the main purpose of his life. If feeding goes smoothly, the straightforward approach to food that he learns in his first year will continue into childhood. If feeding a healthy baby or child becomes a problem, it means something has happened to disrupt this natural process.

• UNDERFEEDING AND OVERFEEDING •

Physically, there are two kinds of feeding problem. Underfeeding, or malnutrition, occurs in deprived societies where food is scarce. It's also found in affluent societies like ours. Too much choice is worse than too little, and a child may miss out on the simple, natural food he needs for healthy growth and development.

It's natural to be concerned if your child seems to eat too little. Nutrition is important, and feeding is central to mothering. Because of this, many mothers instinctively encourage their children to eat more. In fact, overfeeding is much more common in our society than underfeeding. This is not just in spite of mothers' feelings that their children don't eat enough for their health; it can also be a result of those feelings.

• HOW PROBLEMS START •

Babies are sometimes fed too much milk, especially when their mothers are concerned about how much they eat. It's common for babies to be introduced to solids very early, again perhaps in order to feed them more, at a time when their digestive systems are still immature and unable to cope. Commercial baby food contains lots of unnecessary sugars and starches. A baby who is urged to

11

eat when he isn't hungry, or one who expects all food to be bland, sweet and smooth, is primed to become one who rejects his meals. The more his mother urges, the more he refuses. This is how eating problems begin.

Parents concerned about nutrition try to limit sugary, fatty snacks, like sweets and crisps, because they know these spoil the appetite for meals and contribute nothing to a healthy diet. What's less commonly known is that milk, a useful and nutritious food, is often the culprit in an eating problem. In older babies and children, too much milk can cause overfeeding if it's taken in addition to meals, and underfeeding if it replaces meals. This frequently happens when milk feeds continue to be taken at night. The milk not only spoils the appetite for meals, it interferes with sleep. A good night's rest makes a big difference to how well a baby eats.

Convenience foods and processed snack foods also complicate children's eating patterns. High doses of sugar cause a surge in blood-sugar levels, followed by a rapid fall, which creates a craving for more sugar. In this way, sugar is addictive. A child who replaces balanced meals with sugary snacks may suffer wildly fluctuating moods and energy levels, swinging between listlessness and hyperactivity. These eating habits, if continued into later life, lay the foundations for eating disorders, especially obesity.

•FOOD AND FEELINGS•

The physical facts of what a child eats, and how much, can't be separated from the emotional associations with food that develop from the day he is born. For an infant, feeding is an emotional experience as much as a physical one. Indeed, for a young baby, there is no difference. His stressful feelings find bodily expression through feeding, sleeping and digestive difficulties.

He takes his whole idea of the world from you, so your attitudes to food and your feelings about it are a major influence on him from the beginning. Food has powerful emotional associations for all of us. When these become exaggerated, such as when food becomes our main source of comfort or pleasure, eating problems are the result. This can happen to small children as well as adults.

Because food is so central to life, and especially to the relationship between mothers and children, eating means much more than the simple satisfaction of hunger. It's also an opportunity for social interaction, and a source of enjoyment. The social dimension of food and the customs surrounding eating are part of how a child becomes part of his family, and his community. Parents guide their children's eating behaviour as part of that process. Problems arise when eating itself – how much the child eats, and what – becomes a matter for a parent's authority and a child's rebellion.

Feeding a child, instead of being easy, simple and natural, can become a family's biggest source of stress. Anxiety about feeding can run so high that it's impossible for anybody to relax. No-one, child or adult, finds it easy to eat well if they can't relax.

Because food has such emotional significance, it is an arena where all sorts of other issues are negotiated and fought out. Parent and child can find themselves locked in a battle of wills, played out over every meal or demand for sweets. If food becomes a source of conflict instead of pleasure, it's a wasted opportunity for everyone, and children are more likely to grow up with difficult feelings about food.

• THE SIMPLE SOLUTION •

The simple solution is to trust your healthy, growing child to eat what he needs to go on growing and being healthy. Provide him with good food, step back and allow him to eat without interference. Stress and conflict of any kind are your enemies if you want your child to eat well. It's a basic rule that the more you worry about a child's eating, the less well he's likely to eat.

Even the smallest babies will indicate clearly that they've had enough to eat for the time being. Allowing a baby to stop feeding when he's had enough, and resisting the temptation to urge him to take a bit more, is the first step on the way to making sure you don't sow the seeds of conflict over food.

As a new parent, you are suddenly faced with the awesome responsibility of taking care of your baby – literally, of keeping him alive – and that may make you anxious about feeding. The practice of measuring your baby's progress by his weight gain can also feel like a judgement of you as a parent. Remind yourself that a new baby is a survivor, but he does have to learn to feed. If he senses anxiety or tension in you, it will be more difficult for him.

Once feeding is well established, and anxieties are soothed by visible evidence that your baby is thriving, it will soon be time to introduce solids. This opens up a whole universe of choices. Negotiating the business of eating throughout babyhood and childhood means adventure, learning, experiment and fun for you both. At times, though, it can also be frustrating, bewildering, infuriating and exhausting.

The simple solution to feeding has two goals:

- To give your baby the best possible nutrition and the best possible feeding experience. That means laying the foundations of a lifelong healthy attitude to food at the same time as building bone, brain, muscle and a strong immune system.
- To make life as easy and pleasant as possible for you. That means removing the source of all unnecessary stress, anxiety, conflict, confusion, misunderstanding, effort and expense.

Many parents share the first of these goals, but they don't imagine it's compatible with the second. You may feel that, if a child is to learn what's good for him, stress and strain are inevitable. But this sacrifice of a harmonious atmosphere is pointless when the only result is a child who finds mealtimes a burden.

In fact, not only are the two goals both desirable and compatible, they actually reinforce each other. Once you know what your baby needs, and what you need, you can balance the two in the simplest possible way.

Whatever the question, the answer will always start with one ground rule: keep it simple. What is quick, easy and inexpensive for you will often also be what's best for your baby.

• HOW THIS BOOK WORKS •
Preparing Yourself

This book begins with pregnancy, because this is the ideal time to consider your own attitudes to food, and how they will influence your baby. Chapter 1 is all about you. Recognizing your own associations with food will reveal the instincts you'll bring to feeding your baby. Your expectations of what, how and how much your child should eat can create problems if they don't match your child's own particular needs. Pregnancy is also the time to decide how you plan to feed your new baby. Chapter 2 discusses how this important decision is made, and offers some fresh perspectives to help you choose.

Breast-feeding

Breast-feeding is often abandoned in the early weeks because difficulties getting started may convince a mother that her baby is not feeding properly. Promoting breast-feeding as the easy, natural, perfect way to feed a baby does women no service when it leaves them unprepared for the challenge which early feeding sometimes presents.

The naturally unsettled behaviour of a new baby trying to adjust to life outside the womb may be interpreted as a sign that feeding is not going well. Advice to persevere does no good when both mother and baby are having an anxious time, and the mother's confidence is being undermined with every feed. It's no wonder that so many mothers become discouraged and switch to the bottle.

The first few weeks of feeding are a learning experience for both mother and baby. Approached in the right way, this stage will be followed by breast-feeding that does live up to its image as easy, rewarding and mutually satisfying. Chapter 3 describes how to get breast-feeding established successfully, while avoiding the common mistakes that can cause problems, confusion and frustration.

Combining Breast and Bottles

The baby who is exclusively breast-fed until he takes all his fluids from a cup is the exception today. The reality is that most babies will have bottles at some stage. Combining breast-feeding with bottles for certain feeds is a practical solution when full breast-feeding is not. It has the advantage of allowing you to continue breast-feeding for one or more feeds a day, sometimes long after you would otherwise have given up.

Combined feeding is seldom recommended, but by following one or two simple rules it can be successful and satisfying for both mother and baby. For many mothers, it's the perfect solution, combining the benefits of breast-feeding with the convenience of bottles. Chapter 4 describes how to do it. It also discusses expressing breast milk to feed in bottles, as well as bottle-feeding from birth.

Reading Your Baby's Signals

Some people prefer to feed on schedule, others on demand. Both have advantages and drawbacks. These are discussed in Chapter 5. Feeding on schedule can help to make sure your baby is hungry enough to feed properly. However, prolonged crying for food can also make your baby too exhausted to feed eagerly when feeding time finally arrives. It also does nothing to build communication between you, and can cause you both to suffer needlessly.

Feeding on demand is the best method when it means what it says, that is, feeding your baby when he needs feeding. Sometimes, though, the swing away from feeding on schedule goes too far in the other direction, and well-meaning mothers feed their baby every time he opens his mouth. Feeding a baby when he doesn't need food is no better for him, or you, than making him wait for feeds.

Your baby's first tastes of solids introduce him to the business of proper eating. Chapter 6 describes how to make sure it's an enjoyable experience for you both. The key is to take the cue from your baby. If he's ready for food, he'll take to it quickly and eagerly. His digestion, his confidence and his attitude to food will all benefit if solid food is delayed until he makes it clear that milk is no longer enough.

Baby Food: Too Much, Too Soon?

Commercially prepared baby food is a useful stand-by for most parents. Nutritionally, a baby who lives on food from packets, jars and tins will not go short. The drawback to most baby food is the opposite: it provides a great deal that your baby *doesn't* need. Manufacturers encourage parents to buy by suggesting that feeding a baby is a complex, delicate business that they understand better than anyone else. This false mystique no doubt plays a part in many parents' feeling that their baby is better off eating products made especially for him.

The simple solution to feeding relies on feeding less, not more. A baby should have milk only until he makes it clear he wants more, usually between four and six months. This avoids sensitizing his immature system to possible allergens, makes sure he's developmentally ready to enjoy eating, and builds confidence and trust in both parents and baby as they discover that he can make his needs clear.

When he does need more than milk, simple cereals, fruit and vegetables will provide enough nutrition and variety to keep him going for several months. Most baby food contains a great deal more. Protein is important for growth and tissue repair, so manufacturers name their products 'fish pie' or 'beef casserole' in order to make parents feel that they are buying a nutritious, balanced meal. The truth is your baby does not need animal protein at all, and certainly not when he has only just started eating solid food.

In addition, most baby food includes added starches and sugars. These accustom your baby to bland, sweet tastes and provide cheap calories without educating him about food. Chapter 7 analyses baby food in detail and shows you how to find out exactly what you're buying by looking at the ingredients label, rather than at the name on the package.

What To Eat and When

Chapter 8 discusses meals, snacks, treats and drinks. It explains the importance of building healthy snacks into your child's regular diet. If you expect him to need something between meals, you can carry snacks around with you. This prevents your child's blood-sugar levels dropping too low and the behaviour problems that go with it. It also means you don't have to go into a shop to buy a snack, where your hungry child will be tempted by sweets. It shows you how to make sure your child will happily drink water instead of sugary drinks that spoil his appetite and damage his teeth.

Chapter 9 discusses the whole question of what babies should eat, and when. This sometimes seems impossibly complicated, and no doubt makes many parents feel it's too tricky to feed a baby with home-prepared food. We're told babies can have rice but not wheat, spinach but not tomatoes, fish but not eggs. No wonder many parents give up and decide to let baby-food manufacturers take the responsibility.

Once you know the reasons for these guidelines, you can make up your own mind. On the whole, delaying the introduction of certain foods is a precaution against allergy or infection. Some food groups, such as wheat and dairy products, are known to trigger allergies in children who are prone to them. Complex proteins, including those in formula milk, can leak from the immature gut of very young babies and provoke an allergic reaction. For these reasons, as well as many others, it makes sense to delay solids for at least four months, and to keep your child's diet as simple as possible for as long as possible.

Avoiding Conflict Over Food

The seeds of many eating disorders, including obesity, are sown in infancy. Food carries powerful emotional associations for all of us, and what those are depends a great deal on our childhood experiences. Chapter 10 shows how it happens that, while doing their best to feed their children, many parents find themselves locked in conflict over food. This creates unhappiness, tension and bad feeling on both sides, and turns meals into battlegrounds.

Eating difficulties don't just happen, and a child doesn't just decide to rebel over food. Very often, fights over food are not really about food at all. The answer is sometimes to step back, ignore what your child is eating, or not eating, and pay attention to something else.

Food Problems: Non-food Solutions

Problems over food can often be solved by taking food out of the picture altogether. From the first days of life, food and satisfaction are very closely linked. It's important to give your baby attention and interact with him in other ways as well. This shows him that satisfaction isn't always accompanied by food. Children learn very quickly that food is a powerful means of attracting attention. Refusal to eat can be a demand for attention; so can pleading for sweets. A child who has plenty of non-food satisfaction is less likely to use food in this way.

It's all too easy to get caught up in an argument about food and overlook the real, underlying issues. It helps to ask yourself one or two key questions when you are mystified by your child's behaviour over food. 'What is going on here?' 'What is this really about?' The answers you come up with should help you take charge of the situation in a way that allows your child to relax and eat when he's hungry, instead of using food as a way of getting attention.

A question that goes to the heart of tension over food is: 'Who is in charge of what?' You are responsible for choosing, providing and preparing the food you want your child to eat, and giving it to him in a way that makes eating easy. That does not make you responsible for his eating, too. It helps to think of it as your job to provide good food at appropriate times, and his job to eat it. Giving your child control over his own eating is the quickest route to no-fuss feeding.

The Best Approach

The best way to tackle eating problems is to make sure that a problem never develops in the first place. The answer is to allow your child to eat what he needs, while preventing him from having too much of what he doesn't.

This can mean overturning some deep-seated ideas, such as feeling it's your duty to make your child clear his plate. But the rewards are enormous. If food has never been a matter for dispute, it will not occur to your child to conduct his power struggles with you over dinner. If he argues about bath-time instead, at least you won't be worrying about his health. There is no reason why mealtimes with children should not be pleasant occasions, where everyone can satisfy their own appetite in peace. You have every right to insist that they are, for your own sake as well as your family's.

Chapter 11 consists of a set of golden rules, a handful of simple principles to guide you through feeding from birth to childhood. Chapter 12 contains recipes, tips and suggestions for nutritious, healthy home-prepared food, much of it ready to eat in less time than it takes to open a packet.

* * *

Food is important, but it's not worth arguing over. Childhood is short enough. In the time you save by not fussing over food and trying to persuade your child to eat it, you could do something you both enjoy. That's just as good for health as eating your greens, and it makes better memories.

1

BEFORE BIRTH
Preparation for Parenthood

SURPRISING as it may seem, there is a great deal you can do before your baby is born to make sure feeding goes well. Understanding how your baby learns to feed, how she's affected by what she eats, how to avoid feeding problems, how your influence will shape her attitudes to food and her health into adult life – all this will make a tremendous difference to your feeding relationship from earliest infancy throughout childhood. It's also much easier to think about it now than it will be later on, in the midst of the day-to-day demands of looking after your baby.

Parents often say it's only when their children are older that they see clearly, for the first time, what was going on during the struggles over food in the early years. It doesn't have to take that long. With some practical knowledge and common-sense tactics, you can embark on parenthood well prepared to give your child the best possible start.

Your baby will have a lot to learn as she adjusts to life outside the womb, and you will have everything to learn about her. If you're prepared for a two-way learning process, you'll take the ups and downs of feeding your baby in your stride. But if you cherish a hazy, rose-tinted image of blissful bonding, the reality can come as a bit of a shock. If you're a new parent, and it's all uncharted territory, it can feel uncomfortably like the blind leading the blind. However, there's plenty you can do to help things settle down quickly and smoothly. Your reward will be feeding that's easy and automatic – even blissful.

Pregnancy is also the perfect time to take a good long look at yourself, as your own eating habits and attitudes towards food will have a major influence on your baby. There's increasing evidence that eating disorders have their foundations in infancy and childhood. A child's earliest experience of food, and her associations with eating, will powerfully affect her own adult attitudes to food, and to feeding her own family.

•WHAT YOU EAT•

You already know that you need to eat well in order to meet the tremendous demands of nourishing your growing baby in the womb, but it is also important for you to build up your reserves of strength and energy in preparation for her arrival. Becoming a parent is exhilarating, challenging and exhausting. Eating well and getting plenty of rest are among the best things you can do to prepare yourself.

While your hormones are fluctuating, during pregnancy and after the birth, a good diet will help stabilize your metabolism. It will also boost your immune system, to help you cope with the demands of birth and motherhood without becoming run down or ill.

If you eat enough of the right kind of food in pregnancy it will help your baby grow fit and strong. We know more and more about the importance of the period before birth, and recent studies have shown that nutrition in the womb is a significant influence on health throughout life.

There's no doubt that eating well in pregnancy is one of the best things you can do for your baby. But you can do more than that. You can also give her the best possible start on a lifetime of good eating habits. At the same time, you can make sure that feeding your baby, and later your child, is easy and pleasant for you. From the beginning, you can lay the foundation of good eating habits and clear communication that will stand you both in good stead for years to come.

•YOU AND FOOD•

Start with considering honestly your own feelings about food. These will be a powerful influence on your child, whether you like it or not, so this is a good time to start sorting them out, and thinking about what you want your baby to learn from you.

Clare's little boy, Alexander, is five years old. Clare says Alexander won't eat vegetables, and can detect even tiny amounts sneaked into pasta sauce. While she's saying this, Alexander is eating a large helping of mashed potato, so clearly he will eat some vegetables. Clare remembers refusing to eat vegetables herself as a child, so, she says with a smile, 'Perhaps it's genetic.' Later, she expresses horror at the idea of giving children cauliflower cheese. 'But cauliflower is disgusting!'

As a good mother, Clare would like Alexander to eat his greens. But at a deeper, more personal level, she identifies with his rejection of some vegetables, since she felt the same way as a child. Because of this fellow feeling, Alexander is not convinced by Clare's assurances that vegetables are a good thing. Her unconscious influence on him, through her own attitudes and feelings, is stronger than the conscious messages she sends.

★ ★ ★

This is just one example of the way eating patterns tend to run in families. If you remember food being a battleground in your own family, it's not surprising if tension colours your feeding relationship with your child. If you have a love-hate relationship with food, or a pattern of overeating followed by dieting, or if you've ever had any kind of eating disorder, your own complicated feelings about food will be stirred up as you feed your baby, and may be passed on to her. A recent study of mothers with eating disorders showed half had children with low weight or emotional problems.

If mothers were aware that the seeds of eating problems were being sown, they could take steps to change things. But it usually happens without mothers realising it. Pregnancy, before you have to tackle actually feeding your new baby, is the perfect time to pay some attention to yourself, in a way that will be of real benefit to your baby.

Food has three basic functions in society:

● To satisfy hunger.
● To provide the focus for social gatherings.
● To give pleasure.

Some people's feelings about food are no more complicated than that. If that describes you, you are unlikely to become tense about food when you have a child. You will tend instinctively to adopt a relaxed, straightforward approach, and this will be picked up by your baby. But if food has all sorts of other associations for you, if it carries lots of emotional baggage and stirs up anxiety, it will be more difficult for you to be relaxed about feeding your baby. Being aware of this is the first step to sorting it out.

• ASSOCIATIONS WITH FOOD •

Women, especially, often have complicated relationships with food. Whatever your personal experience, some of the reasons for this are common to all women in our society.

- There is a social and sexual emphasis on the shape of our bodies, in particular how slim they are.
- Food is closely tied to women's' historic domestic role, giving it a part in our female identity.
- Feeding is a central element of mothering. How you were fed as a child affects your feelings about food and feeding. This emerges more strongly when you become a mother yourself.

Food has powerful emotional associations. Because of this, emotions, especially ones that may be difficult to acknowledge directly, are frequently expressed through food.

- **Power and control:** A woman who resists eating tempting food for the sake of her figure feels a powerful sense of control over her body. A mother who wields a rod of iron in the kitchen may be expressing a need to feel in control in some area of her life. Trying to make a child eat, or unreasonably denying a child food, is a form of power struggle. To take this example to the extreme, anorexia nervosa has been described by sufferers as giving them a satisfying sense of mastery over their bodies, at a time when they feel powerless and out of control in the rest of their lives.
- **Punishment and reward:** If you are on a diet, you may 'punish' yourself for a lapse by being stricter than ever about what you

24

allow yourself to eat. Or, after a success, you might reward yourself with a food treat. Similarly, children are often refused treats as punishment, and rewarded with sweets. This can create a deepseated feeling that food carries a moral judgement.

• **Comfort:** As babies, we took comfort along with our milk. It is natural to associate food with comfort, pleasure, and relief from hunger and thirst. There is even evidence that certain foods, notably chocolate, chemically enhance mood. Problems arise when food becomes our main or only source of comfort, especially when emotional closeness is in short supply. (Think of the traditional fondness for nursery food among men who went to public school.) Finding non-food comfort treats for yourself – a bubble bath, or snuggling up under a soft rug with a magazine – will help you find different ways of offering comfort to your child without always resorting to food.

• **Conflict and anger:** People who enjoy cooking and preparing food find pleasure in using it to express love and care. Equally, food can be withheld or managed in a way that sends the opposite message, especially when it's difficult to express anger directly. A love-hate relationship with food can reflect feelings of conflict within yourself. Ambivalent feelings about our children, which all parents experience from time to time, may also find expression through feeding.

• **Self-image:** How we eat, what we eat, whether or not we cook, the role food plays in our lives – all this is part of how we see ourselves. A mother who prides herself on providing good food for her children may feel personally rejected when they don't eat it. Instead of concluding they're not hungry, she may feel it's her mothering, even herself, that they're rejecting.

A lot has been written about women's relationships with their bodies, and how eating disorders often have their roots in an obsession with body image and slimness. We are appalled when we hear of adolescent girls with anorexia nervosa, or seven-year-olds wanting to diet, so as to look like a 'Barbie' doll. We worry that television, magazines and toys send the wrong messages to impressionable children about their bodies.

The truth is that by far the most powerful influence on a child's early eating habits is what she learns at home. Inappropriate use of food for emotional reasons, thoughtless feeding and overfeeding can all leave a lifetime's legacy of food problems in their wake.

Later, of course, your child will strike out on her own path, and experiment with food, as well as everything else, in ways you probably won't like. But while you are the main influence in her life, the best thing you can do is to use your influence for good. That means laying a solid foundation of good nutrition and sensible attitudes. It will stand her in good stead, both physically and mentally, even if it doesn't always seem like it to you at the time.

If your own relationship with food is complicated, naturally it's much more difficult to keep things simple for your child.

• DIETING •

Many women spend much of their adult lives on a diet, or at least wishing they were thinner. For them, food can become a constant and terrible dilemma. They crave food, but as long as they deny themselves, they're winning the battle. When they succumb to temptation, though, pleasure is mixed with guilt and a sense of failure.

A simple piece of cake may be loaded with conflicting meanings. It represents the enemy, but it promises comfort, consolation and satisfaction. It stands for desire as well as denial, success as well as failure.

If you are an habitual dieter, pregnancy can come as a blessed relief. It's the one time of your life when you're actually forbidden to diet, because it could deprive your growing baby of essential nutrition. If the feeling of being given permission to be fat by pregnancy is irresistible, you may decide to go on a nine-month binge and eat everything in sight. Why not, since you will have to lose weight after the birth, anyway? There are several reasons why this is not a good idea.

- What you need in pregnancy is lots of healthy, nutritious food. If you binge on cakes, chocolate and chips, you will eat less of the food that you and your baby really need.
- If you put on lots of unnecessary weight, your pregnancy will be more uncomfortable. It also puts extra strain on your heart, causing raised blood pressure, which is not good for you or your baby.

26

- Apart from the health risks, the extra weight will still be there after the baby is born. Breast-feeding consumes enormous numbers of calories, and will, by itself, get rid of most of the fat deposits naturally laid down in pregnancy. But it can't deal with an extra 2st (12.7kg). Dieting while breast-feeding will deprive your baby of vital nutrition. Even if you bottle-feed, you will need energy and strength to recover from the birth and look after your baby. You will have quite enough to cope with without worrying about your weight.
- Pregnancy is the time nature gives us to prepare for motherhood. It is the perfect opportunity to sort out your own eating habits, not only to nourish your unborn baby, but also to give her the benefit of a straightforward approach to food from the start. If you have unresolved eating problems of your own, it will be hard for your baby to develop good feeding habits. She will instinctively copy your attitudes and behaviour.

• HEALTHY FOR WHO? •

Healthy-eating guidelines advise adults to reduce the amount of fat in their diets and increase their consumption of dietary fibre. Initially recommended for those at risk from heart disease, low-fat, high-fibre diets are now considered healthy by most people. Because of that, it's easy to assume this eating pattern must be good for children too.

In fact, adults and growing children have completely different nutritional needs. Babies and children are building bones and brain, as well as muscle, and expending enormous energy in activity. Because they are small, they eat relatively little in proportion to their energy needs. To keep their metabolism stable and meet all the demands of their growing bodies, it's important to provide the right kind of food.

A low-fat, high-fibre diet is completely inappropriate for babies and small children. Fat plays a vital role in their diet. Certain vitamins are only soluble in fat, and fat also provides concentrated calories in small amounts. Current recommendations are that children should have full-cream milk until they are at least five years old.

The fats in nutritious food such as milk, yoghurt, cheese and butter are good for your baby. The ones to avoid are unnecessary extra fats, found in snacks such as crisps and chocolate. There's no point in choosing low-fat yoghurt if your child also has lots of fatty, sugary snacks with little nutritional value. It's much better to provide full-fat products that satisfy the appetite until the next nutritious meal or snack.

High-fibre food provides bulk without many calories. This is the exact opposite of what growing children need, with their high energy needs and small stomachs. It may also cause stomach upsets. A child will get all the fibre she needs from fruit, vegetables and cereals, including bread.

• YOUR CHILD'S SECRET GROWTH PLAN •

Children who are genetically programmed to be small people frequently cause anxiety, because they eat less than their parents expect them to. This is especially difficult for parents who have hearty appetites themselves. It can take a long time to realize that a child is simply small, and eating appropriately for her lower growth needs, not starving herself. Parents may be even more confused if their baby was big at birth.

Lucy's older daughter, Emma, weighed 8lb (3.6kg) at birth. Her growth curve, however, gradually began to level off and, by the time she was six months old, it was causing concern at the baby clinic. Lucy was told to feed her more, and bring her back to be weighed in two weeks. 'Although I had been a health visitor for five years, I was in a complete state,' remembers Lucy. 'It undermines you like nothing on earth when your baby doesn't put on weight. I would burst into tears at the thought of trying to feed her. I felt sure the doctor was going to tell me off and make me feel a failure as a mother. The less Emma ate, the more tense and anxious I got.'

Emma has since grown into a healthy, slim, small eight-year-old. 'She wasn't meant to grow fast,' says Lucy. 'She was born big, but she's programmed to be small.'

This happens because birth weight is determined by a different genetic programme from eventual adult size. There's evidence that birth weight is influenced by information carried in the mother's eggs. Your size as an adult, however, is determined by genetic information from both parents.

There's not necessarily any relationship between where a baby falls in the range of healthy birth weights and her eventual adult size. A man of 6ft 4in (1.9m) may have entered the world at 6lb 8oz (2.9kg), or, like Emma, an 8lb (3.6kg) baby may grow into a small person. When your baby is born, you don't know how she's going to turn out. A healthy baby knows better than you do how much food she needs.

Barbara's husband is very tall, but their son, Andrew, is tiny. At seven years old, he's the smallest boy in his class. When he was a toddler, food was a daily battle. Andrew just did not want to eat more than a few mouthfuls, and he and Barbara were on a constant collision course about it. Now, Andrew's parents have decided he takes after his paternal grandfather, and they accept he's a small child with a small appetite. They look back on their constant confrontations over food as a waste of time and energy.

Provided with a variety of nutritious food, a healthy child will always take what's right for her needs. You can relax and trust her to eat appropriately without pressure from you.

• PREPARATION FOR PARENTHOOD •

The standard image of pregnancy used to be a soft-focus picture of a woman knitting in a rocking-chair, wearing a negligée and a dreamy smile. These days, you're more likely to be in leggings, tramping round the shops. Babies are a boom industry, and manufacturers have deliberately created links between buying their products and taking good care of your baby.

Shopping may provide a way of thinking about your baby which comes more easily in today's world than sitting and knitting. But whatever you decide to buy for your baby, remember her primary needs will be love and milk. She will need to be kept safe, warm, clean and dry. Nothing else will matter to her. All she really needs is your care and attention, and the more rested and relaxed you are, the easier these will be to give.

By all means, buy things that give you pleasure, or that will save you time and effort. But as far as your baby is concerned, the best investment you can make is time and thought spent on preparing yourself to meet her needs and guide her through her adjustment to the world. It's easy to lose sight of yourself as you rush around trying to get ready, but, for your baby, *you* are what it's all about. You are her whole world. Take good care of yourself, and you'll be taking good care of your baby.

FEEDING PLAN FOR PREGNANCY

▶ Treat pregnancy as your opportunity to prepare yourself for motherhood. That means taking time to think about how you plan to feed your baby, and what you want her to learn about food and eating.

▶ Think about your own attitude to food, remembering that your child will learn more from the way you are, how you feel and behave, than anything you deliberately say or do.

▶ Don't overeat because you are pregnant. This can cause problems for you and your baby, and it means missing the chance to work out a sensible approach to eating which you'll be able to pass on to your child.

▶ Eat lots of nutritious, healthy food, to help your unborn baby grow strong, and to boost your own strength and vitality in preparation for birth and motherhood.

▶ Plan to make the most of the few years when you control what your child eats, so as to lay a sound foundation of good nutrition and sensible attitudes.

▶ Remember a low-fat, high-fibre diet, while healthy for adults, is inappropriate for growing babies and small children.

▶ Trust your healthy baby to know her own needs. You don't know what size she's programmed to reach, so trust her to eat the right amount of food, and don't worry if it's less than you expect.

▶ Don't get too caught up in trying to provide everything on the market for your baby. What she really needs is your loving care and attention. Try and take good care of yourself so that you can take good care of her. Nothing else matters nearly as much.

2

YOUR FIRST
BIG DECISION
Breast, Bottle–or Both

O F ALL the dozens of choices before you, there is only
one decision that really needs to be made before your
baby is born, and that's whether you're going to breast-feed or
not. It's a big decision, and an important one, and that can make
it intimidating.

There are fashions in infant feeding like everything else, and
the advice of the day can feel like a barrage of pressure, just when
you're most vulnerable and uncertain. The present emphasis on
'breast is best', while based on sound facts, goes too far when it
makes women anxious. It can even encourage bottle-feeding, in
order to take the pressure off the woman herself.

Everyone is different, and everyone has different needs and
priorities. What's important is that your decision is your own, and
not one you feel pushed into.

• HOW THE DECISION IS MADE •

- **Doing what's usually done in your family:** If you were breast-
fed, and your mother enjoyed it, you have a positive role model
who may be able to give you valuable support and encourage-
ment. If your mother tried breast-feeding and quickly gave it
up, however, you will have less confidence, and probably less
support, as she may instinctively expect your experience to
mirror her own. On the other hand, if you were bottle-fed, it
may feel right to do the same with your own baby.

  There's no doubt it makes life easier when you do what your
family expects you to. It takes courage to make your own

decision. If it's different from what those around you expect, you need to be determined, and to make sure that you have support from outside your family as well.

- **'Breast is best':** If you believe breast-feeding offers your baby the best start, but feel unsure about doing it, discuss your feelings with health professionals before your baby is born. Ask for support in getting feeding established. If you want to breast-feed, you should. Get good advice, and keep an open mind. You can't know what it's like until you try. It may go smoothly and be a source of great satisfaction to you both.

- **Not being tied to the baby:** If you plan to go back to work within a few weeks of the birth, or you want to share feeding duty, you may feel it would be better to bottle-feed from the start. In fact, once breast-feeding is established, you can adapt it to suit yourself, by replacing certain feeds with a bottle, or expressing milk for feeds you won't be giving. Not being with your baby all the time doesn't mean you can't breast-feed if you want to.

- **Having tried and failed to breast-feed before, or seen others fail:** This can be very discouraging. First-time mothers often embark on breast-feeding with high hopes, assuming that, because it's natural, it will be easy. Sometimes it is, but often it takes several weeks for you and your baby to learn the ropes. If you aren't given the information, help and support you need to continue, and you're both relieved to switch to a bottle, the experience can deal a severe blow to your confidence. Naturally, that will put you off trying again. Seeing another mother struggle can have the same effect.

   Remember that no two experiences, or babies, are the same. Anxiety and tension over a first baby may itself create problems. If you don't see yourself as the serene 'earth mother' many people associate with breast-feeding, don't worry. You can find your own style. Even if you are habitually an anxious person, stress need not interfere with breast-feeding.

- **Just not liking the idea of breast-feeding:** The public emphasis on breasts as sexual objects, which goes hand in hand with a more mysterious, private image of breast-feeding, can make it hard to imagine your breasts nourishing a baby. Or, if you feel uncomfortable and unattractive in pregnancy, you may be eager to regain control of your body after the birth. If you are anxious for control, bottle-feeding, which lets you measure the exact amount of milk your baby is taking, can seem more appealing.

Sometimes, these feelings are a reaction to the upheaval in your own identity caused by pregnancy and birth, and they change as you gain confidence. The truth is, whatever method you choose to feed your baby, it is impossible to be totally in control when you are a parent. Having a baby means embarking on a new and intense relationship with another person. In conceiving a child, you have started a process that has its own momentum. You, and your life, will change through that process, however you approach it.

Drawing on Other Mothers' Experiences

It may help you to consider some other mothers' experiences when thinking about what you want to do.

Catherine is a mother of three. She struggled to breast-feed her first baby for six weeks, then switched to a bottle. The younger two were bottle-fed from the start.

'I really wanted to feed my first,' she remembers, 'but it was hell. I didn't have enough milk, and he was always crying, and we were running around with electric breast pumps, and the stress was unbearable. As soon as I switched to the bottle, everything was fine. He ate, he slept, he stopped crying. I couldn't face all that again, so we bottle-fed the other two on schedule from day one.

Catherine's husband was involved and helpful. He borrowed the electric breast pump from the hospital, and they reached the decision to switch to the bottle together. He then took charge of night feeds for all three babies, and his experience convinced him that bottle-feeding was the way to get babies to sleep through the night. (Later, he discovered that breast-fed babies can, and do, sleep through the night as early, and as easily, as bottle-fed ones. How the baby's sleep is handled makes much more difference.)

Dividing the care of their babies with her husband has suited Catherine, although she has some regrets about not succeeding at breast-feeding. She says her husband is better at managing small babies than she is. His confidence with them was perhaps enhanced by his positive experience of bottle-feeding, while Catherine's may have been dented by her feelings of failure.

Well-meant advice from a husband, mother or other relative is often a factor that convinces a woman who wants to breast-feed to give it up. In the end, it is your body, your experience, and your decision. Those around you should support you in that decision, whatever it is, although of course this can be impossible for them if you are not sure what you want yourself.

Eleanor is a mother of four. She made the decision to bottle-feed when she was pregnant with her first baby, and has never reconsidered it. These were the reasons she gave:

'Breast-feeding just doesn't appeal to me. I don't want to do anything that would exclude my husband. I'm having a maternity nurse at night, so this way I can get an unbroken night's sleep, as she can do the night feeds. As a bottle-fed baby myself, I feel happy about it, as my health is excellent and I feel deprived of nothing. And I want to go on a strict diet when the baby is born, to get my figure back as quickly as possible. You can't diet if you're breast-feeding.'

Eleanor reported with amusement that the stresses of early parenthood had taken the form of disputes with her husband over the exact amount of formula their baby had consumed. Her husband, apparently, did not write down the amount on the chart as precisely as Eleanor and the maternity nurse did.

Of course, no-one else will ever do things exactly your way. Some parents find it less stressful to have different tasks that they can appreciate each other for doing, rather than trying to share everything.

Arguing over details can also be a way of expressing other anxieties. Realistically, it makes no difference whether a healthy baby takes ½oz (14g) more or less. A new baby's contentment depends a great deal on a feeling of closeness and security with his mother. A partner's support plays a crucial role in this. It can make it possible for a mother to give her baby this feeling, even when she feels vulnerable and uncertain herself.

Eleanor's first baby had frequent colds and minor infections. This is less likely when a baby is breast-fed, as breast-feeding boosts a baby's immature immune system. Her second baby, however, was more robust. She went back to work full time when each one was six weeks old, but gave up work altogether when her second child was two years old.

'I always felt my work was central to who I was, and part of how my husband saw me and what he found attractive about me. I didn't want to lose that, so I kept mothering at arms' length,' she says. 'Now, I feel confident that I'm still me, and a mother as well.'

Never forget that your first baby has the job of teaching you how to be a mother. It's a big shift in your identity, so it's best to make allowances for it, and to let it take its natural course. Keep an open mind as far as possible, as you may find hard and fast decisions made during pregnancy appear in a different light once you and your baby have got to know one another.

Eve put her baby to the breast immediately after a Caesarian section under epidural, and never looked back. She had ample milk, and expressed and froze the surplus, so that when she was not around her baby could have breast milk from a bottle. It was hard for Eve to understand other mothers' difficulties in getting breast-feeding established, as she had no experience of any problems herself.

36

She fed her baby on a four-hourly schedule, which usually seemed to satisfy him. But although feeding was straightforward for Eve, her baby found it difficult to relax and sleep. It's often taken for granted that a well-fed baby will sleep well, but a baby may find it hard to settle for all sorts of reasons.

Sometimes the mother of a restless, anxious breast-fed baby decides to switch to the bottle, believing it will make him more content. Depending on the reason for his discontent, it may help, or it may not. Changing the way a baby is fed won't be the solution if what he really needs is more closeness and reassurance, so that his feeds are more satisfying, emotionally and physically, making it easier for him to relax and sleep.

Lara was determined to breast-feed her first baby, and persevered in spite of several breast infections, treated with antibiotics. Each course of treatment dealt a blow to Lara's immune system, and was followed by another infection. With her second baby, she had no sign of mastitis until he was five months old, and starting solids. She decided gradually to phase in a bottle for certain feeds, to reduce her milk supply and the chance of infection.

'I dreaded the infections returning with my second baby,' she says, 'but I decided to try breast-feeding and see what happened. As it turned out, it went well for much longer than I expected, and I can still give him some breast-feeds. If it had been as bad as the first time, I would have given up altogether. I'm glad I didn't have to.'

Sarah has two sons. She was anxious over her first baby, who was born at a stressful time for the family. She remembers a feeling of chaos and being unable to concentrate on feeding her son. He, however, seemed to look after himself, took what he needed, and was content.

'I used to look at him and think "I don't know how you put up with it",' she says. 'I was so grateful to him for managing to cope and feed, when I was in such a muddle that I hardly knew what I was doing.'

Her second son, however, was restless and difficult to satisfy, even though Sarah was more experienced and confident by the time he was born. Now nine years old, the older boy remains placid and tolerant, while the younger, aged seven, is still volatile and restless.

Sarah's experience suggests that your baby's personality may be a powerful influence on his feeding experience. It helps to remember that there are two people involved in every 'feeding pair'. Your baby's temperament may make feeding easier, or more difficult. Whatever happens, it's not all your fault!

Leaving Your Options Open

If you're uncertain of the best method for you, a good solution is to decide to commit yourself to breast-feeding for the first six weeks, and then look at the whole picture again. This leaves all your options open, and has certain particular advantages:

- It gives you and your baby the experience of breast-feeding, which is one of the best and quickest ways to build communication, closeness and trust. Skin-to-skin contact is reassuring for your baby, and feeding is something you share and have to negotiate together right from the start.
- It boosts your baby's immune system.
- It avoids introducing any artificial formula into her diet in the early weeks. This helps to protect against allergies, because it avoids sensitizing her system to potential allergens in formula milk before her immune system has a chance to develop resistance.
- It allows your baby to learn how to breast-feed efficiently, and you to learn how to feed her, before introducing the new experience of a bottle, if you so choose, at a later stage.

Introducing a bottle before breast-feeding is well established leads some babies to reject the breast. Milk is delivered faster from a bottle, and the baby doesn't have to work nearly so hard to feed. If he is not yet an expert breast-feeder, he may decide he can't be bothered to make the effort to feed from the breast.

- It allows you to develop your own pattern of mixed breast- and bottle-feeding, if that's what suits you. This is only successful if breast-feeding is well established first. (See Chapter 4.)
- It means you can continue breast-feeding for as long as you and your baby are enjoying it. Even if this eventually comes down to just one feed a day, it can be a source of great pleasure for both of you. When the anxiety of the early weeks is over, the closeness and communication of breast-feeding really shows.

Pregnant women are often presented with the choice between breast- and bottle-feeding as if it is black or white, either/or, one or the other. It is seldom pointed out that this is only true for the first few weeks and, even then, not absolutely. The odd bottle does not mean the end of breast-feeding, even for a new baby, although it will make it more difficult to get it running smoothly.

The idea of combining breast- and bottle-feeding is sometimes dismissed as impossible. This may lead women who can't commit themselves to months of exclusive breast-feeding to opt for the bottle from the start. But there's no reason why that should mean not breast-feeding at all, or stopping breast-feeding just as it's becoming easier.

As countless mothers have discovered for themselves, a mixture of breast and bottle works perfectly well, once breast-feeding is established. This method allows breast-feeding to continue when you return to work, or decide for any reason to introduce a bottle for some feeds, even if you don't express breast milk.

Combined feeding appeals to those mothers, perhaps the majority, who would like to breast-feed but, for one reason or another, are unable to do it exclusively until their baby can drink from a cup. This is the exception today. But that doesn't mean you or your baby should miss out on breast-feeding.

The key to successfully combining breast- and bottle-feeding is to get breast-feeding established first. How to do this is the subject of the next chapter.

PLAN FOR DECIDING HOW TO FEED YOUR NEW BABY

► Spend time thinking about it, and be aware of the influence of your family. Make sure that what you decide is what you really want. Everyone is different, and it takes courage to make your own decision.

► Ask your partner and family to support you in your decision, especially if it is different from what they expect. Talk it over with them so that they understand why it's important to you.

► If you believe breast is best for your baby but feel unsure about doing it, discuss it with a midwife or health visitor before your baby is born. Ask for help in getting feeding established.

► Don't assume that, because breast-feeding a baby is natural, it's automatic. It's a skill you have to learn, and so does your baby. Some mothers and babies seem expert from the start; others need a few weeks to sort themselves out.

► Remember that your new baby will need lots of closeness, to establish trust and communication between you. The skin-to-skin contact of breast-feeding is an easy and effective way to achieve this.

► Keep an open mind. Change is inevitable when you have a baby, and hard and fast decisions made now may appear in a different light once you and your baby have got to know one another.

► Combining breast- and bottle-feeding is one way to have the best of both worlds. If this is what you would like to do, you will need to establish breast-feeding first.

3

HOW TO ESTABLISH
BREAST-FEEDING

LIFE with a new baby revolves around feeding. Feeding is the major issue of your baby's life, and therefore of yours. Her early progress will be measured by her weight gain. For all these reasons, if feeding goes well and her baby thrives, a breast-feeding mother may take the credit, and bask in a warm glow of approval and success. If, on the other hand, a mother and baby struggle to get feeding established, it's very hard for the mother not to blame herself.

Because we regard feeding as the essence of motherhood, failure in this department can feel like failure as a mother. This is no doubt at the root of some decisions to bottle-feed. But it's wrong to see breast-feeding as an examination that you either pass or fail. It's a skill to be learned by practice. You and your baby may take to it immediately. It's just as likely that one or both of you will take time to get the hang of it. Although early difficulties are common, they are hurdles you can overcome together, not signs that you're no good as a nursing mother.

Be prepared for it to take a week or two to learn the ropes, and don't expect instant success. You may be lucky and wonder what all the fuss is about. If not, don't worry. There are lots of things you can do to make it easier.

• EARLY DAYS •

Your baby needs to learn how to feed and, just as with children and adults, hunger is the best incentive. From your point of view, the more confident you are, the easier you'll both find it. Trust and confidence grow on both sides as you establish communication. Her need for food is the basis of the first vital exchange of signals between you.

Your baby cries for food. You respond by offering the breast. She feeds eagerly, which is gratifying for you. Replete, she relaxes into a calm state, the frantic anxiety of hunger gone, and will sleep if she needs to. It's obvious that you've supplied everything she needs, and her contentment is visible proof of your good mothering.

That's the image of feeding most of us have in mind, if we think about it at all, before we start. It's the reality too, once feeding is established. It can be a great source of pleasure and enjoyment for both of you. Sadly, many mothers give up before they reach this stage. They make the effort, but they miss out on the reward.

Without the right kind of support and help in sorting out early problems, it's easy to jump to the conclusion that you haven't enough milk, and offer a bottle instead. A restless and unsatisfied baby is terribly demoralizing for a mother devoting herself to her care. You will be told to persevere, but your baby's discontent can feel like a reproof to you as a mother, and this can undermine your confidence so badly that you haven't the heart to go on.

What you want to establish is a clear rhythm of hunger, feeding, satisfaction and sleep. Hunger is a new and distressing experience for your baby, who has been accustomed to a constant supply of food in the womb. She needs to learn the connection between the relief of hunger pains and her own eager sucking. At the same time, she learns her cries of distress will be met with food and comfort. This pattern, regularly repeated, becomes her earliest experience of the world as a safe, secure and predictable place, and of her mother as a reliable source of satisfaction.

From the day your baby is born, you can start learning to recognize her hunger cry. This makes a tremendous difference to how quickly and smoothly early feeding is established.

• THE HUNGER CRY •

The hunger cry has a sharp, urgent, frantic sound. The unpleasant and unaccustomed sensation of hunger overwhelms your baby, and she cries as if her life depended on it (which, of course, it does). When you hear it, it's hard to mistake. Rather than wondering what the matter is, you're more likely instinctively to drop everything and feed her.

It's unlike the fretful or grizzly cry of fatigue, or the whimpering and wailing of discomfort. However, there is one trap to look out for. Hunger pangs probably feel the same as indigestion to a new baby, so her cry may sound the same. It's easy to be misled into feeding her again, overloading her digestive system and increasing her discomfort. That's why a gap between feeds is essential. You will soon come to recognize your own baby's particular 'language' of noises. But initially it's a process of experiment for both of you.

Some mothers' instinct is to offer the breast whenever their baby cries, rather than listening to her, looking at her, and trying to work out what she needs. They reason that, if she's hungry, she'll feed. If not, the breast will comfort her. A crying baby will often accept the breast, even if she's not hungry, because sucking is soothing and pleasurable. The breast may seem the answer, whatever the problem.

It's true that the breast is a wonderful way of giving your baby reassurance and emotional succour as well as food. Since she spent the first nine months of her life inside you, it's no wonder skin-to-skin contact comforts her, and helps her feel integrated into her bewildering new world. But offering a feed every time your baby cries does create problems.

- It makes it hard for you to learn clear communication with your baby, in a way that allows you to respond appropriately to her needs, as and when she has them.
- It makes it hard for your baby to learn to communicate her different needs to you.
- It sends the message to your baby that she can't manage without the breast, even for a short time. This does nothing to boost her confidence in her growing ability to manage for herself, such as going to sleep when tired, or waiting a little while for food.
- She will feed even when not hungry, because sucking is pleasurable. The extra food may overload her digestive system and cause discomfort.
- The pain of indigestion may feel like hunger, so her cry may sound the same. But more food will make matters worse.
- If your baby is never really hungry, she may never take a proper feed. Breast-feeding is hard work for your new baby, and she needs to be hungry to make the effort.

- If your baby doesn't suck strongly, your breasts may not be stimulated to make enough milk.
- If your baby snacks when peckish, she may be restless: never really hungry, but never replete and able to relax into sleep. She may suck just enough to soothe her hunger pangs and drop off. But after a short while, hunger will wake her again.
- This can create a pattern of snacking and napping which may lead to a prolonged night-feeding habit.

The way to avoid all this is to wait until you're sure your baby is hungry before you feed her. When you think she's hungry, you can confirm it by gently stroking her cheek. She'll respond by lunging towards you and opening her mouth wide, ready and eager to feed.

• HOW TO BREAST-FEED •

There is a strong sucking reflex present at birth, so the sooner you can put your baby to the breast the better. If she isn't ready to make the effort to suck strongly, she'll still be learning about feeding when she nuzzles and explores.

It's best to have a midwife with you the first few times, to make sure you and your baby are well positioned to make feeding easy. Before every feed, check that you're both comfortable.

- Shake tension out of your arms and drop your shoulders. Any tension in your body will be picked up by your baby and make it difficult for her to feed.
- Support your arms and your baby with pillows, so you can relax without hunching over. When sitting in a chair, make sure that your feet are flat on the floor and your spine is straight.
- Bring your baby towards you, don't lean towards her. Position her so that you are chest to chest.
- Make sure she opens her mouth wide and gets a good mouthful of breast as well as the nipple. This is called the 'latch'. It makes sure that the baby 'milks' the breast properly with her jaws, and it helps to avoid sore nipples. There is usually a twinge as your baby latches on, but this should go away as she begins to feed.
- Watch your baby to make sure she's feeding properly. You will

be able to see her jaws working, and her ears wiggling as she swallows. Some babies' foreheads wrinkle up and down. It should be obvious that your baby is working hard, 'munching' at the breast and swallowing frequently.

- Allow your baby to feed from one breast as long as she wants to. Some babies only ever take one breast at a time; others quickly learn to empty both breasts. If she feeds from one breast only, remember to offer the other first at the next feed.

- Only feed for as long as your baby is feeding properly. It's the quality and efficiency of the feed that counts, not how long she spends at the breast. A baby who has mastered the technique will take 90 per cent of her feed in the first three minutes. While you are learning the ropes, the whole business of feeding, winding and changing should still take less than an hour.

- When your baby slows down or stops, she has had as much food as she needs for the moment. She may still enjoy sucking for pleasure, but she's no longer feeding in earnest. A few minutes of this is enjoyable for both of you, but don't allow it to go on too long, or your baby will become overfull and uncomfortable, and you'll get sore nipples.

Don't give *any* bottles while you are establishing breast-feeding. This may be difficult if the early feeds are unsatisfying for you both, and your baby seems hungry and fretful. Some mothers and babies get the hang of breast-feeding immediately; others take a bit longer. If you are struggling, 'top-up' bottles can seem to be the answer, but they should be avoided if you want to breast-feed.

Bottle-feeding requires a completely different technique. The baby doesn't have to work as hard, and the milk is delivered faster. While she's learning to feed, even one or two bottles can mean a set-back to her progress. More than that and she may become reluctant to breast-feed at all. (Later, a fully breast-fed baby may reject a bottle altogether, so if you plan to use a bottle for some feeds, there is an optimum moment to introduce it. See Chapter 4.)

• A STORY WITH A HAPPY ENDING •

I wish I had known all this when my baby was born. Our early experience was a mixture of determination and ignorance on my part and confusion on the baby's. Looking back on it, I had hoped for the best without any real confidence or knowledge. When my doctor asked if I planned to breast-feed my baby, I replied: 'I'd like to, if I can.'

Family history plays a part in breast-feeding, as in everything else. You may inherit a tendency to be a 'good cow', as it used to be called, or not. You may also pick up a feeling about breast-feeding, that it is easy or difficult. My mother, a doctor, struggled to breast-feed both her babies for a few weeks before switching to a bottle. 'I was a dreadful cow,' she said.

My baby was put to the breast soon after birth, and praised for her willingness to suck. But during our time in hospital, I also sometimes gave her a bottle after her breast feed. She was alert and hungry, and my milk didn't come in until the fourth day. I was not discouraged from doing this. No one told me that my milk would come in faster if my hungry baby strongly stimulated my breasts at frequent intervals, and formula feeds were readily provided.

It certainly didn't occur to me that my baby should scream with hunger: I wanted her to be satisfied and content. We had a blissful, peaceful time. My baby actually left hospital having gained weight, unusual in the first few days after birth.

Our problems started on our first night at home. No matter how often I tried to feed her, she couldn't settle. I began to think she must be hungry, and at 6 a.m. I cracked and gave her a bottle. She fed eagerly and went straight to sleep. Confused and exhausted, so did I.

Instead of improving, her breast-feeding got worse. She cried for the breast, but treated it more as somewhere to snuggle and doze than the place to work at filling her tummy. At ten days old, it seemed she already knew there were easier ways to do that. She would drop off to sleep contentedly, then cry when removed.

I read the books, consulted the clinic, telephoned doctors and breast-feeding counsellors, all to no avail. My mother, knowing all this struggle, anxiety and exhaustion wasn't good for me or the baby, suggested I switch to a bottle. But in spite of everything, I loved breast-feeding, and didn't want to give it up.

At that point, we had a stroke of luck when Lucy Smith arrived as our health visitor. Lucy was the first person to recognize what was wrong and show me how to sort it out. She explained that my baby had simply not learned to breast-feed. There were three main reasons why:

- She had been given top-up bottles when she should have been working hard at learning to breast-feed, so she didn't learn to make the effort breast-feeding required.
- Concerned that she was hungry, I had been putting her to the breast every time she cried, so in fact she wasn't hungry enough to make the effort to feed properly.
- My milk supply was low because my baby wasn't sucking strongly enough to stimulate my breasts to make more.

We started from scratch. Lucy banned the bottle, and showed me how to tell when my baby was truly hungry. This also allowed the baby to experience the sensation of hunger, and to let me know clearly when she did. The advice to feed as often as the baby wanted had encouraged me to feed too frequently. This had not helped my baby learn to recognize when she needed food.

We worked on lengthening the gap between feeds, so the baby began to get properly hungry, and clearly demand food. Then she fed strongly, was satisfied, and slept while my body made more milk. Within a week, we were in calmer waters. We went on to breast-feed until my baby gave it up, aged ten and a half months.

At my six-weeks' check, I told my doctor about my difficulties establishing breast-feeding. I suggested that I should have been told not to give bottles in hospital. 'Well, she was hungry, and you can't starve a baby,' she replied.

It seemed the struggle at home was the price I had paid for those peaceful few days in hospital. Without the bottle, my baby would have cried a lot more as she became hungry enough – starving, if you like – to make the effort required to feed properly. In her second two weeks, we had to learn what we should have been learning from day one, as well as unlearn the bad habits we had already acquired.

It made me wonder how many mothers give up breast-feeding when they don't want to, because the right kind of help and support isn't available. Sleepless nights and unsatisfying feeds are a terrible combination. Exhaustion and anxiety are coupled with confusion and feelings of failure. 'Not enough milk' seems to be the obvious conclusion. The bottle offers instant relief, for both mother and baby. But as I discovered for myself, even when beginning breast-feeding isn't easy, if you want to do it, you can.

• YOUR MILK SUPPLY •

Milk is produced automatically in response to the hormonal changes of pregnancy and birth. The first substance produced is colostrum. Colostrum is high in antibodies, and helps protect your new-born baby from infection.

Colostrum is all the food a healthy new-born baby needs. Some babies are sleepy at first and seem to wake up and start feeding in earnest when the milk comes in. Others may be restless, unsettled and anxious in the first few days. They may be slow to work out that the painful new sensation of hunger can be soothed by vigorous sucking at the breast. This is the time to keep calm, even though your baby's unsettled behaviour can be distressing. Remember, she has to learn, and you can help her.

On about the third day, your milk comes in, and your breasts feel very full and tender. Now you need your baby to suck well if you are not to become engorged. This is what happens when your breasts are so full of milk that they become hard and painful.

Once the milk has come in, the amount produced is regulated by your baby's appetite. Your body makes more milk while your baby is feeding, to replace what she takes. Mothers who want to produce more milk are advised to feed more often, but this works only if your baby feels vigorously hungry enough to suck strongly at each feed.

A baby who does not suck strongly will not give the breasts the stimulus they need to make more milk. It is your baby's appetite which regulates the supply, not the number of times she is put to the breast. As always, the simple solution is to respond to your baby, rather than trying to stay one jump ahead.

Mastitis is a painful infection that commonly occurs in the early weeks of breast-feeding. It can be caused by engorgement or a blocked milk duct, or infection may enter through a cracked nipple. You feel feverish, as if you are getting influenza, and a red, shiny, painful patch appears on the breast. Mastitis responds rapidly to treatment, but it is important to keep feeding your baby or engorgement will make the problem worse.

Some mothers produce copious quantities of milk (one described it as 'like turning on a tap'), and the evidence of plentiful supplies boosts their confidence. Others may always worry whether their baby is getting enough. One rule of thumb is that if your baby has six or eight wet nappies a day and gains weight, she is getting enough.

Often, it's the most attentive, concerned parents who have feeding difficulties with their baby. These parents sometimes find it hard to trust their baby to manage for herself. In their efforts to help their baby, they may actually make life more difficult for her.

By wanting to take the best possible care of our babies, we can make the mistake of doing too much for them. This interferes with their own ability to adapt to smooth rhythms of eating and sleeping. It may seem tough when you're a new parent hovering anxiously over your baby, but the best thing to do is let her learn to tell you when she needs food. Problems are much less likely if you put your baby to the breast when she's hungry, and find other ways of soothing and settling her when she's not.

• WAYS TO SETTLE A RESTLESS BABY • BETWEEN FEEDS

- Go outside. The change of air often makes crying stop as if by magic. Wrap your baby in a blanket and go. It's only for a few minutes. The aim is to break the tension for both of you.
- Walk around with your baby, experimenting with how she likes to be held. Some babies enjoy lying face down on your arm, or hanging over your shoulder. The pressure on their tummies may help with indigestion.
- Swaddle your baby. Lay her on a flannel sheet or shawl and wrap her firmly, like a parcel. Include her arms, and tuck up her feet. This seems to reassure new babies, perhaps by reminding them of the snug surroundings of the womb. But remember that new-born babies can't regulate their own temperature, so make sure that she is not too warm.
- Lay her face-down on your knee and pat her back.
- Talk and smile, with your faces about 12in (30cm) apart. She will enjoy the sound of your voice and practise focusing on your face.

- Make sure she's not too warm. New babies are unable to regulate their temperature, and easily become too warm or too cold. Babies are frequently overdressed in heated homes and shops.
- Rock in a rocking-chair.
- Dummies help if a baby is obsessed with sucking. Sterilize them for young babies. Don't worry if you don't like dummies; it needn't become a habit. You can stop it when the passion for sucking abates, some time after your baby starts solids.

Once breast-feeding is established, you can combine it with bottle-feeding. Many mothers do this successfully, although it's not usually presented as an option. How to do it is discussed in the next chapter.

PLAN FOR ESTABLISHING BREAST-FEEDING

▶ Put your baby to the breast as soon as possible after birth. Have a midwife with you for the first few feeds, to check your positioning and make sure your baby is latched properly on to the breast.

▶ Always shake tension out of your arms and shoulders before picking up your baby. Make sure your shoulders stay dropped down during the feed. Your baby will pick up any tension in your body and that will make it difficult for her to feed.

▶ Learn to recognize your baby's hunger cry. It has an especially sharp, urgent sound. Feed her when she's definitely hungry, and try other ways of soothing her when she's not.

▶ Confirm the hunger cry with the 'rooting reflex': when you stroke her cheek, your baby will lunge towards you and open her mouth wide.

▶ Watch for signs that your baby is feeding properly. She should munch at the breast, and swallow frequently. You will see her jaws working, and her ears wiggling as she swallows.

▶ Allow your baby to get properly hungry between feeds. This will help her learn an efficient feeding technique, and stimulate your breasts to make plenty of milk.

4

BOTTLE-FEEDING AND COMBINED FEEDING

IN A PERFECT world, all mothers would breast-feed and enjoy it, and all babies would thrive and be content. But even in societies where breast-feeding is universal, babies still die when breast-feeding fails. Luckily for us, we have a choice. If breast-feeding is impossible or undesirable for any reason, we can be confident that our babies will flourish on bottles of infant formula.

The simple solution is all about choice. Clear information makes decisions easier, and helps what you choose to work well for you. This chapter describes three choices:

- Expressing breast milk to be given in bottles.
- Replacing certain feeds with bottles of infant formula.
- Bottle-feeding from birth.

In the first two options, the bottle should be introduced once breast-feeding is well established.

- Bottle-feeding requires a completely different technique from breast-feeding, and it's important not to confuse your baby by introducing a new feeding method before he has mastered the first one.
- Your milk supply should be stable before you begin to tinker with it. Your body is flexible and will adapt to the patterns you choose, but the system needs to be up and running smoothly first.
- Because feeding from a bottle requires less effort from the baby, if it's introduced before he has become a proficient breast-feeder, he may lose the motivation to breast-feed and prefer the bottle.
- Seeing your baby gain weight on breast milk alone will boost your confidence as a nursing mother. If bottles of formula are

introduced too early, you may never feel sure that you can provide everything your baby needs.

- If you leave it too long before introducing a bottle, your baby may be so set in his ways that he refuses it altogether. He will take it eventually, but it will be more difficult for him to accept the idea and learn the new technique it requires.

• BREAST MILK IN BOTTLES •

If you express breast milk, your baby can have some of his feeds from a bottle while remaining fully breast-fed. You can express by hand or by using a pump. Manual and battery-operated pumps are widely available. Some women who express routinely find it worthwhile to hire an electric breast pump.

It's possible to express milk, store it in the office fridge and take it home to be fed to your baby the next day. This keeps up supplies and allows you to return to full breast-feeding at weekends. Many mothers express milk occasionally, perhaps so that someone else can give a feed when they need to rest.

Apart from times when your baby would have fed, you can also express between feed times, or if there is any surplus at the end of a feed. Breast milk can be either stored in a covered container in the fridge for twenty-four hours or frozen for up to one month.

There is a knack to expressing breast milk. Some mothers find it easy; for others, it's slow going. Although it's not difficult, many women find it more trouble than it's worth. For them, combined feeding may offer a practical solution.

• COMBINED FEEDING •
A PRACTICAL SOLUTION

Some women find the total responsibility of breast-feeding too demanding. Many enjoy it, but find the pressures of their lives mean they can't fully breast-feed for long. Working mothers can't be with their baby all day.

Although it's seldom presented as an option, combined feeding is a good compromise. It makes breast-feeding practical for mothers who consider it ideal, but impossible for them. However enthusiastically mothers are encouraged to breast-feed, the baby who is exclusively breast-fed until he can take all his fluids from a cup is the exception today. Reality dictates that most babies will have bottles at some stage.

This does not mean you might as well bottle-feed from the start. Your baby will continue to benefit from breast-feeding as long as you keep it up. The younger he is, the more benefits it has. Colostrum, the fluid produced in the first few days after birth, is high in antibodies and boosts your baby's resistance to infection. Because of this, even breast-feeding for as little as a week is valuable. In addition, his digestive system is underdeveloped at first. Breast milk is the only food perfectly adapted for his immature gut.

Once breast-feeding is established, bottles can be introduced for the feeds you choose, and your milk supply will adapt accordingly. This gives you and your baby the satisfaction and benefits of breast-feeding, along with the flexibility and convenience of bottles.

Breast Before Bottles

Although combined feeding is very common in practice, some people consider it impossible. This is because bottles can put a baby off breast-feeding altogether if they're introduced before he's become an efficient breast-feeder. He may quickly decide that the bottle is an easier source of food, although he still enjoys comfort-sucking and nuzzling at the breast. This is the worst of both worlds for the mother, who spends her life either preparing bottles or putting him to the breast, half the time not even knowing which he wants. Her milk supplies will dwindle as demand is increasingly reduced.

Don't introduce a bottle from the start to get your baby used to it, perhaps because you plan to go back to work. This is likely to bring breast-feeding to an end sooner than you want. Wait until breast-feeding is well established. Your baby may resist the bottle at first, but he will take it once he realizes that it's food and he's hungry. It helps if someone else can give the bottle, so the breast isn't available.

Be prepared for fuss, struggle and splutter the first few times. Your baby may give the impression he doesn't want the feed. He does; it's just that at first he has no idea what to do with the bottle and doesn't know what to make of the new taste. Be patient and reassuring, and he'll adapt quickly.

The Top-up Trap

Top-up bottles are a trap to avoid. The baby takes his breast feed, but seems still hungry. Suspecting she may not have enough milk, his mother tries offering him a bottle as well. The baby takes it. He settles down, and his mother heaves a sigh of relief. It seems like a success all round.

Unfortunately, the result will be less breast milk for the next feed. Now that some of your baby's needs are being met by the bottle, your body gets the message that demand has been reduced, and makes less milk. This is how your milk supply dries up when you wean your baby off the breast. In this case, though, it's not what you want. At the next feed, there will be insufficient to satisfy your baby, and another top-up bottle will be needed. It's a vicious cycle. Discouraging for the mother and confusing for the baby, the muddle usually ends in full bottle-feeding before long.

You may regret not having enough milk, without realizing that you actually send your body instructions to make less milk when you supplement breast feeds with formula milk.

Keeping Up Supplies

To be successful at combined feeding, give no bottles at all until breast-feeding is well established. Then introduce a bottle for certain specific feeds. As long as your baby still sucks eagerly at the breast for his other feeds, your body will quickly adapt to the new, longer gap between breast feeds. Your milk supply will be reduced in total, but the amount available to your baby at his remaining feeds will be adequate.

After breast-feeding is well established, it takes just a couple of days for your body to adjust to changes in demand. When your baby has a growth spurt, for example, he will want to feed more frequently. This stimulates the breasts to make more milk, in response to the increased demand.

In the same way, as your baby sleeps for longer and longer

periods at night, your breasts will adapt to the changing feeding pattern. Some mothers believe their milk will dry up if they stop feeding at night. This is not so. My own baby slept for twelve hours a night from the age of three months, and continued to be fully breast-fed until she started solids, two months later.

When is the Right Time to Introduce a Bottle?

There is no particular age when a baby is ready to accept a bottle for some feeds; it varies with the baby, the mother, and the way feeding goes. Breast-feeding is well established when your baby is feeding efficiently, and when you feel confident about the whole process, from your baby's hunger cry to the let-down reflex that gets the milk flowing into his mouth.

Most people don't reach this degree of confidence on both sides for about six weeks, although some mothers and babies are ready sooner.

- The first two weeks are commonly a confusing period while you, your body and your baby get used to breast-feeding.
- Over the second two weeks, things usually settle down, with both of you getting the hang of it.
- After that, it's helpful to give yourself a week or two when all is going well and your confidence grows as you see your baby feeding and growing.

How to Start Combined Feeding

Introducing your baby to combined feeding is similar to the way you would wean him from the breast onto a bottle or cup if you were planning to give up breast-feeding. The only difference is that, when weaning completely, you want your milk supply to dry up, while, for combined feeding, you don't. You can decide which feeds will be breast and which bottle, but it's important that it's a regular pattern, or your milk supply won't be able to adjust.

You can replace breast feeds with up to three bottle feeds a day and continue to breast-feed for the remaining feeds, usually one in the morning and one or two in the evening. The system allows you to keep the breast feeds that suit you for as long as you like, or until your baby gives them up of his own accord. For some mothers, this means eventually cutting down to just one or two breast feeds a day. Many continue to enjoy the early morning feed, in particular, for some time after other breast feeds have tapered off. It can be a special, quiet time of closeness with your bigger baby, who is showing so many new signs of independence from you in other ways.

Alternatively, if complete breast-feeding is difficult after the early months, you may decide to replace just one breast feed a day with a bottle feed. It's common for your milk to be low towards the end of the day, for example, if you're tired and finding it difficult to relax. Giving a bottle at this time may turn a stressful feed into a pleasant one for both of you and allow breast-feeding to continue for the other feeds.

Whether you intend to replace one, two or three breast feeds with formula milk, you need to do it gradually, so that your body has a chance to adapt to the new pattern. Start with replacing the feed which seems least important to your baby. If you plan to replace a second breast feed with a bottle, allow a few days for your body and your baby to get used to the first adjustment before repeating the process.

Don't worry if your baby splutters and coughs. At first, he will try to breast-feed from the bottle, which doesn't work at all. Remember breast-feeding requires more vigorous sucking than bottle-feeding. He has to learn a new technique, as well as adapt to a different taste. It might help to use a soft latex teat. Large, hard, silicone teats will be even more alien to a breast-fed baby.

At first, your breasts may become uncomfortably full at the time of the dropped feed. If this happens, express just enough milk to make yourself comfortable. Don't use a pump for this, as it provides too much stimulation. If your baby has bottles while you're at work and you breast-feed at home, you will probably have to express milk at work, at least occasionally. Gradually, your body will adjust to the new pattern.

Once your baby is having some bottles of formula milk, he may become thirsty. Breast milk varies in composition from day to day, from feed to feed, and during each feed. Formula milk doesn't, so offer him some cooled, boiled water between feeds, especially if the weather is warm.

• BOTTLE-FEEDING FROM BIRTH •

If you decide to bottle-feed from the beginning, your doctor or midwife will give you appropriate advice. Your baby will have no trouble adapting if he has a bottle from the start. It is worth taking some trouble, however, to make sure that the hole in the teat is the right size. Too big, and your baby may cough and splutter. Too small, and he may cry with frustration if the milk is delivered too slowly. You can check by turning a bottle of his usual milk upside down. It should drip out at a rate of several drops a second. You can enlarge the hole, if need be, with a sterilized needle.

Bottle-feeding need not mean that your baby misses out on the closeness and warmth of breast-feeding. You can hold him close, look at him and engage with him just as you would if you were breast-feeding. Always give your baby his bottle in your arms, so you can see how well he is feeding, and when he has had enough. He may choose to take very small feeds frequently at first. Don't worry about this, and don't urge him to take more than he wants. Trust him to know his own needs, and resist the temptation to measure every fraction of an ounce he takes.

Use the bottle for food, and try other ways of soothing your baby when he's restless. (See Chapter 3 for suggestions.) This also allows your baby to take comfort from you, rather than the bottle. If the bottle becomes a substitute for you, your baby may become passionately attached to it. Never let your baby go to sleep with a bottle in his mouth. A small baby could choke. Later, he will become unable to go to sleep without the bottle. Milk also contains sugar, which is bad for his developing teeth.

You will need to sterilize everything for the first few months. Without the antibodies in colostrum, the first breast milk, your baby is more vulnerable to infection. Germs breed easily in milk, so scrub teats and bottles well with a bottle-brush before sterilizing. When your baby starts rolling around on the floor and putting everything in his mouth, sterilizing becomes pointless, but bottles and teats should still be scrupulously cleaned before use.

The easiest system is to make up the day's supply of bottles in one go and store them, sealed, in the fridge. Warm a bottle by standing it in a jug of hot water. Test a few drops on the inside of your wrist; it should feel tepid.

By the age of three months, most bottle-fed babies are having five feeds a day. There's a limit to how much a baby can take at each feed. If your baby has a growth spurt and seems hungrier than usual, and he's already taking a full bottle, you will have to give him an extra feed. This is preferable to introducing solids too early. Formula must be made exactly to the manufacturer's instructions. Never use extra powder, and never add anything, such as sugar or cereal, to your baby's bottles. This puts a strain on his digestive system, and leads to overfeeding.

Let your baby practise taking sips from an open cup from about six months. By nine months or so, when the strong sucking urge abates, a cup of milk can replace the bottle at some or all of his meals. Try and phase out the bottle altogether by about one year. A colourful beaker is a good alternative for outings and bedtime drinks. If bottles are continued beyond the age of one year, they tend to become a firm habit. A baby who would not have missed his bottle at a year will fiercely defend his right to it by the time he reaches two.

FEEDING PLAN FOR INTRODUCING A BOTTLE

▶ Don't introduce bottles too early if you want to continue breast-feeding as well. Before he becomes a proficient breast-feeder, your baby will find the bottle less effort, and may prefer it to the breast.

▶ Once breast-feeding is established, bottles can be introduced for the feeds you choose, and your milk supply will adapt accordingly. This gives you and your baby the satisfaction and benefits of breast-feeding, along with the flexibility and convenience of bottles.

▶ Complete breast-feeding, with no bottles at all, will establish a good milk supply over the first few weeks.

▶ Breast-feeding is well established when your baby is content and feeding efficiently, and when you feel confident about the whole process, including the hunger cry and the let-down reflex. This commonly takes up to six weeks.

▶ Bottle-feeding requires a different technique from breast-feeding, and formula milk also tastes quite different. Because of this, your baby may cough and splutter and appear to reject the bottle at first. Give him time, and be patient and reassuring.

▶ Combined feeding is successful when specific breast feeds are replaced with bottles, but not when bottles are used as top-ups after breast-feeding. This will cause your milk supply to diminish in response to the reduced demand.

▶ Give all bottle feeds in your arms, so that you can see how well your baby is feeding, and give him plenty of closeness and interaction. Let him stop as soon as he has had enough.

▶ Aim to phase out bottles altogether by around the age of a year. After this, the bottle becomes a habit, and your child may refuse to give it up.

5

FEEDING ON SCHEDULE OR DEMAND?

─────── ★★★ ───────

As a new mother, Frances was encouraged to feed her baby, Isabella, on schedule every four hours. For the first few weeks, Isabella was content with this regime. 'It will help her sleep through the night as soon as possible,' Frances was told.

Frances stuck dutifully to the schedule. 'When Isabella cried, I thought she couldn't possibly be hungry if it wasn't feeding time. I assumed it must be something else, and tried other ways to soothe her.'

When Isabella reached three months, a time when many babies have a surge of growth and development and need more milk than before, she suddenly lost 11oz (311g) in weight. Staff at the baby clinic were concerned enough to telephone early one morning to tell Frances to put Isabella on the bottle at once, as it was clear she didn't have enough milk.

Frances didn't want to give up breast-feeding, and her sister pointed out that she would produce less milk if she introduced a bottle, as her breasts would not be stimulated to make the extra supplies Isabella needed. Instead, Frances increased the frequency of breast feeds. When Isabella started solids, she ate eagerly and quickly gained weight.

Isabella is now a healthy three-year-old with a baby brother. Frances blames this upsetting episode on her rigid feeding schedule. 'I was paying more attention to the clock than to my baby. Isabella was doing everything right. Looking back, I can see she was telling me she needed more food.'

'I think she had begun to give up hope. I suppose she realized crying for food was useless. Anyway, she stopped doing it. One day she didn't ask for food for six hours. That was a low point.'

'With my second baby, Louis, I'm more relaxed, and more realistic. I feed him on demand, and he's amazingly easy. He slept through the night much earlier than Isabella.'

Not many babies lose weight as dramatically as Isabella. Frances's experience is an extreme example of what can happen when feeding depends on the clock, instead of on a clear exchange of signals with your baby. Some babies are happy with four-hourly feeding from the start, but they are more the exception than the norm.

• MYTHS ABOUT DEMAND FEEDING •

- **Your baby will be spoilt and expect to get her own way all the time:** It's impossible to spoil a young baby. She has to make a big adjustment, from a continuous supply of food in the womb to learning to satisfy her hunger by sucking. She doesn't yet know how to make unreasonable demands. She can only express her primary needs and feelings. Once she is settled and content, she will be better able to wait for food

- **You will be feeding all the time:** Some lively new babies need feeding very frequently at first. Others are sleepy in the early days and need more frequent feeding later. But if her needs are met, your baby will soon settle down into a pretty regular pattern. Some mothers interpret feeding on demand to mean feeding whenever a baby cries. This will certainly mean feeding very frequently, but it's no more desirable than feeding by the clock. Demand feeding should mean feeding your baby when she needs feeding. If you feed her all the time, she's likely to take more food than she needs and suffer from indigestion.

- **Your baby will go on waking in the night to demand feeds:** She will, if that's what you teach her to do. A baby doesn't always need food, but if she gets it anyway, she will start to expect it. As her digestive and nervous systems mature, she becomes able to sleep for long periods at night. Breast-fed and demand-fed babies do this as early, and as easily, as bottle-fed and schedule-fed ones. How content and satisfied your baby feels, and how her sleep is handled, are much more important.

- **It makes it impossible to get into a routine:** Routine works best when it emerges naturally. You have needs, and so does your baby. You have achieved the ideal balance when nobody feels deprived. Feeding your baby on demand doesn't change her basic needs, but lets you respond to them appropriately. This frees you both to move on together, instead of struggling over whose needs come first.

    Imposing a routine on a very young baby serves no purpose. The quickest route to a settled baby is a satisfied one, who feels her needs are met as she has them, and who quickly learns she can trust you to listen to her and help her.

    New mothers are often anxious to stay in control of things, as Frances described. The experience of becoming a mother and suddenly acquiring responsibility for a human life can be over-whelming. It's natural to want to clutch at anything that seems to offer order or structure. But when this prevents you getting to know your baby and being in tune with her, as Frances found, it will actually slow down the process of adjustment for both of you.

Schedule feeding is tough on babies whose digestive systems are not set on a four-hourly cycle from day one. It is not a system that would have been devised by mothers themselves. Its advantages are that it allows medical professionals to give clear instructions about feeding, and it provides a programme when you don't yet feel confident that you can trust your baby to communicate her needs. It also provides a timetable, an image of order and control which can be reassuring for mothers who fear being overwhelmed by the demands of a new baby.

• MYTHS ABOUT SCHEDULE FEEDING •

- **It's the best way to regulate a baby's digestive system:** The best way to regulate a baby's digestive system is for her to get really hungry between feeds, so that she sucks strongly, feels satisfied and is able to relax until her tummy is empty again. This also stimulates the breasts to make supplies suited to the baby's needs.

Four-hourly feeding can ensure a baby is hungry enough to feed properly. But a baby does not have to be left to scream with hunger to achieve this. The answer is to feed her when she's hungry.

- **Crying is good for her lungs:** This has no basis in fact. It was probably said in order to console mothers distressed by their baby's howling for food. A normal baby's lungs develop along with the rest of her. How much she cries has nothing to do with it.

A baby who cries a great deal is communicating distress. If she is hungry, tired, uncomfortable or anxious, helping her will do much more for her development, and for your relationship, than ignoring her for long periods, which can only give her the impression that the world is a cruel place.

- **It shows the baby who's boss:** The stage when it becomes necessary to make it clear that you're in charge, as every parent discovers, is toddlerhood. As one mother put it, she suddenly discovered a capacity for laying down the law which she didn't know she had. You don't need to enforce the limits until your child needs to test them.

Setting out to teach rules to a small baby is as misguided as trying to teach her to read. Of course you're the boss. To your baby, you're the whole world. Feeding her when she's hungry meets her needs and helps her feel secure. That's an appropriate way of being in charge.

A baby whose needs are satisfied is usually less demanding than one who's constantly thwarted. For example, there's evidence that babies who are held a lot become better sleepers than others.

- **The doctor advised it, and he knows best:** When your baby is ill, she needs medical help. Even then, most doctors recognize parents' instincts as an important guide. No-one knows your baby better than you do. A mother whose baby was born in the 1960s tells of weeping as she watched the hands on the clock inch towards feeding time, while her baby howled ravenously. She knew perfectly well she was hungry, and she longed to feed her.

She endured it because she had been told it was best for her baby. She wanted to be a good mother, and she thought that meant doing as she was told. It's difficult to develop an easy, close relationship with your baby when you're both under this much stress.

Today, the pendulum has swung in the opposite direction, and mothers are encouraged to follow their instincts. This is fine if you're confident about looking after your baby, an experienced mother, or surrounded by helpful supporters. Many new mothers, though, repeat that being told to do what they feel is right increases anxiety.

'Do what you think best,' I was told at the baby clinic.

I felt like wailing: 'But I don't know what's best! I've never done this before. I don't want to get it wrong. I need guidance.'

What helps is practical information that allows you to build communication and trust in your relationship with your baby. Confidence grows naturally from the experience of getting it right. Only then is it possible to follow your instincts in a way that genuinely feels best, for your baby and for you.

•HOW OFTEN SHOULD YOU FEED? •

Although feeding on demand is usually recommended these days, some mothers prefer to feed on a four-hourly schedule. If you do this, it's important to watch and listen to your baby closely for signs that she's not getting enough. Babies vary in their needs. While a big, placid baby may be content with four-hourly feeding from the start, a smaller, more anxious one may only be able to manage for two or three hours.

Problems can crop up as your baby grows and needs more food than before. The only way your body gets the signal to make more milk is when demand is stepped up. That happens when your baby feeds more frequently than before. If her schedule prevents her taking the extra feeds she needs, your milk supply may become insufficient, and she may lose weight or become fretful.

Many mothers don't realize that too-frequent feeding will also result in less milk if your baby isn't hungry enough to feed properly and stimulate the breasts to make more supplies. It's best to let your baby set the pace, always remembering to make sure she is hungry before you feed her.

In the first couple of weeks, while you are both learning the ropes, feeds may be as frequent as every couple of hours. But it's still important to make sure your baby is feeding properly at each feed, and to try other means of soothing her before putting her to the breast if she has fed very recently or doesn't seem really hungry. When your baby's hunger is satisfied, her feeding will slow down and she may stop and start for a while.

This is the time to give her a few minutes of sucking for pleasure, also known as 'comfort-sucking'. Too much of this, however, will confuse your baby and encourage her to treat the breast more like a dummy than a source of food. While she's learning to breast-feed, this won't help.

- The extra food she takes in can cause indigestion.
- If she sucks for relief from indigestion, she takes in yet more food, which makes matters worse.
- Lazy nuzzling, rather than feeding, will not stimulate the breasts to make more milk. Make sure she feeds properly first.
- Constant sucking is a quick route to sore nipples.

Aim to gradually lengthen the amount of time between feeds. Try to make it a minimum of an hour and a half, even if you feel your baby has had an unsatisfying feed and needs another. It helps your baby establish a rhythm if she's given a chance to get properly hungry between feeds, and it gives your body a break. As things settle down over the first few weeks, even if your baby is still feeding very frequently, the gap between her feeds should now start getting longer.

• THE CLOCK AND THE BABY •

Sometimes, a mother will be advised to throw away the clock, so as to be guided entirely by the baby. If your life lets you ignore the clock, this is fine. Most people find it impossible, however, and the suggestion can reinforce the impression that demand feeding is for those with nothing else to do.

There's no reason why you shouldn't look at the clock and at your baby.

- It helps to build up a picture of your baby's behaviour if you notice that her feeds are gradually getting further apart, or that she's feeding more frequently today than yesterday.
- It confirms the emergence of a feeding pattern as your baby becomes more settled. You will notice that she is hungrier at some times of day than others. Some babies seem to need a 'double feed', two feeds quite close together, in the evening. It's as if they're stoking up for the night ahead.
- You may find your baby arrives, of her own accord, at a pattern very similar to the one she would have had if fed on schedule from the start. This will have been achieved without distress, and with the positive benefits of communication and mutual satisfaction. Now you can tinker with her feeding times to suit yourself.
- If it's only an hour since her last feed, it's unlikely your baby is hungry. She may be uncomfortable, anxious or tired. You could try other methods of settling her, as described in Chapter 3. If she really is hungry, nothing but food will help.
- It's interesting to see how, as she becomes an efficient feeder, her feeds get shorter and shorter. Once breast-feeding is well established, babies take most of their feed in the first three minutes.
- You will come to know roughly when you can expect your baby to need a feed, and work around that when planning your day. As long as your baby is with you, unexpected hunger need not be a problem. Once breast-feeding is established, if you need to leave her, she can have a bottle of expressed breast milk or infant formula.

PLAN FOR FEEDING ON SCHEDULE OR DEMAND

▶ Remember it's impossible to spoil a new baby. Once she's settled, she'll be better able to wait for a feed.
▶ Don't leave your baby screaming for food until the clock says it's feeding time. She can't tell the time, and will become exhausted and distressed.
▶ Don't feed your baby whenever she cries. This can muddle communication, and cause digestive problems.

▶ Feed your baby when she's hungry, and experiment with other ways of soothing her when she's not.

▶ A satisfied, contented baby is likely to be less demanding than one whose demands for food are routinely thwarted.

▶ Babies breast-fed on demand can, and do, sleep through the night as early, and as easily, as those bottle- or breast-fed on schedule. How your baby's sleep is handled makes much more difference.

▶ Trying to imposing a routine on a baby who is still adjusting to the world doesn't work. First, she needs to learn that you can be trusted to understand and satisfy her needs.

▶ The quickest route to a settled baby is a contented baby. Some babies need to be held and cuddled more than others.

6

INTRODUCING
SOLIDS

B Y THE TIME your baby is old enough to start eating solid
food, you will know each other quite well. He will be good
at letting you know when he is hungry, and you will be tuned in to
his signals and respond to them appropriately most of the time.
Once milk-feeding is going smoothly, you have successfully negotiated the first big issue of your lives together. You will have noticed
growth spurts (often around six weeks, and again at about three
months, although individual babies vary), and the increased
demand for food at these times.

Starting solid food is simply an extension of these patterns.
The day comes when your baby is no longer satisfied with milk
alone. The key to successfully introducing solids is to let your baby
tell you when this time has arrived.

Don't start your baby on solids simply because he has reached
the minimum age recommended. Your baby is an individual, and
the best possible time to introduce solids is when he is ready for
them. Only he can tell you this, and if you give him the chance, he
will. Trust him to do it, and trust yourself to recognize his needs.

The way he will let you know he needs more than milk is similar to the way in which he has demanded more food during growth
spurts in the past. This time, however, more milk won't be the
answer. If your baby of four to six months old starts taking more
milk than before and, no matter how much you give him, it does-
n't seem enough, he needs to start on solid food. But if he's sleeping
through the night and seems satisfied with five or six milk feeds a
day, he is still thriving on milk alone and there is no need to start
solids just yet. You can leave the timing completely up to him.

If he suddenly goes back to demanding seven feeds a day, and
waking from hunger in the night, he is telling you he needs more.

Choosing the right time to introduce solid food means watching and listening to your baby and following his cues. Be guided by his signals, not his age. The simple solution is truly baby-led, responding to his needs as he has them.

What is the advantage of waiting for the baby's signal? Some parents, perhaps not sure their baby will recognize his needs and communicate them clearly, perhaps just anxious to do the right thing, believe they should start solid food at the time recommended by their doctor, health visitor or baby-care book. It may seem better to leave the decision to the 'experts'. In fact, allowing your baby to decide for himself when he's ready has real benefits for both of you.

- He will take to solid food more enthusiastically if it comes in response to his own need, rather than appearing out of the blue. It makes it seem his idea, rather than yours, and that's always a good approach.
- It contributes to the trust between you. You discover you can depend on your baby to tell you what he needs, and he learns he can rely on you to meet his needs. Starting solids is an opportunity to reinforce confidence in each other.

Fashions in the 'correct' age to introduce solids have fluctuated more wildly than most baby-care advice over the years. A century ago, it was left until babies were a year old. In the 1950s, solid food was introduced at six weeks or even younger, and bottles of formula were thickened with cereal. We now know there are many reasons why solid food should not be given to very young babies:

- Their immature digestive systems are put under unnecessary strain by having to cope with solid food. It can cause tummy upsets or constipation.
- Allergies may be triggered by introducing complex proteins while the immune and digestive systems are immature.
- It deprives the baby of the experience of recognizing and communicating his needs as he has them, and the boost to his confidence and sense of independence that goes with it.
- Imposing food on him before he's ready for it sows the seeds of resistance to eating. A baby who is ready will be more enthusiastic.

- Research suggests that overfeeding young babies may contribute to obesity and related health problems in adult life.

Unfortunately, starting solids is sometimes used as a measure of babies' progress. Progress is much better measured by your baby's individual development, his healthy appetite, and his ability to know his own needs and make them clear. Rather than giving him what you think he needs, you can best encourage his progress by helping him experience his own changes.

The drawbacks of giving solid food too early are now widely recognized, and official guidelines on the best age to start have been revised upwards. Only last year, the minimum age was changed from three to four months. All this confusion could be avoided if parents were encouraged to be led by their baby's individual needs rather than by his age.

There's a right time for everything, and a baby who is ready for a new eating experience will show it when offered his first taste of solids. Presented with food he doesn't want, he's more likely to reject it. It sets the scene for future conflict over food if, right from the start, you find yourself urging a reluctant baby to swallow food he doesn't want.

Apart from the physical advantages of delaying solid food until your baby is ready for it, it gets your new feeding relationship off on the right foot, by giving your baby control over his own eating. Having his needs met as they arise is emotionally as well as physically satisfying for your baby. Having new experiences imposed on him when he doesn't want them is merely bewildering.

Between the ages of four and six months, most babies will indicate that they want more food than before. The advantages of introducing solid food at this stage are many, for you as well as for your baby.

- The digestive system is more mature, and the immune system has had more time to develop resistance to possible allergens.
- Developmentally, your baby is far better equipped than before to enjoy the whole process of feeding. He is more able to sit up and participate, even grabbing the spoon.
- This is also a stage of extreme curiosity, when new experiences are likely to be welcomed, and your baby will be delighted with

the discovery that he can use his mouth and hands. Delaying the introduction of solids too long can mean encountering resistance from a baby who has become more suspicious.

• Introduced at the right time, spoon-feeding makes a significant contribution to your baby's development. His growing sense of a separate self, his eye–hand coordination and his manual dexterity are all enhanced. A younger baby is more passive, and receives fewer developmental benefits.

• If your baby is a good four months old before solid food is introduced, you don't need to sterilize anything. Normal scrupulous hygiene is enough.

By six months, most babies need more than milk to fuel their tremendous growth and development. Increasing activity and mobility means their calorie needs are higher. A baby will take matters into his own hands if need be. One fully breast-fed baby girl of nine months crawled off, took a pear off her father's plate and ate it. 'Oh,' said her mother, 'it looks like she's ready for solids.' Many babies will grab food off their parents' plates from around six months onwards, given half a chance.

Some people enjoy offering a young baby tastes of different foods, to see what he likes. This is not a good idea until your baby is accustomed to a variety of foods. The reason for introducing solid food should be to satisfy your baby's increased appetite, not to introduce variety into his diet. There is plenty of time for that later on. The new experience of spoon-feeding is quite enough novelty for a young baby to cope with at first, and there is no benefit to be had from offering different tastes at this stage. In fact, it can do positive harm, as the complicated proteins in different foods can trigger allergies. Keep it simple, and take it one step at a time.

• INTRODUCING SOLID FOOD •

An ideal first food is baby rice. It is the purest of the grains and the least likely to cause any adverse reaction. Mix it with expressed breast milk, your baby's usual formula milk or boiled, cooled water into a rather runny porridge – remember your baby will try and suck it into his mouth. It should be tepid, the same sort of temperature as his usual milk feed.

You will need a small, flattish spoon with no sharp edges. Hold your baby on your lap, or put him in a lean-back canvas chair if he's comfortable there. If he's already sitting strongly, he can go straight into a high-chair.

Don't choose a time when your baby is tired, as he needs to be ready for a new experience. Mid-morning is many babies' best time. If he's frantic with hunger, giving him a milk feed first should help. Give him only half his usual amount before offering the solid food.

Sometimes, a baby will seem hungry only an hour or two after his milk feed. Then you can try offering the food first, followed by a milk feed. This will become his mealtime pattern for the next few months.

Offer your baby a bit of baby rice on the tip of the spoon. He will lick and suck it at first. Before long, he will be opening his mouth eagerly in anticipation of the spoon. As soon as he loses interest, stop. He may take just a couple of tastes the first few times, but be guided by his appetite and enthusiasm. You don't want him to get the idea that feeding is something being done to him against his will.

One meal a day is enough for the first few days, while he comes to terms with this new experience. If he is keen and seems unusually hungry later in the day as well, mid-afternoon, ideally after a nap, is a good time to introduce a second feed.

Give him nothing but baby rice for the first few days. Then start introducing new foods, one at time, allowing two or three days between each one. This is so that, if your baby does have an adverse reaction to anything, it will be clear which food has caused it.

Fruits and vegetables are ideal first tastes, but avoid citrus fruits and tomatoes as they are too acid. Thoroughly ripe, sieved banana is a traditional weaning food. Ripe, sieved pear and puréed stewed apple are good, too. Root vegetables, such as potatoes, sweet potatoes, carrots and parsnips, are fine first vegetable choices, as are pumpkin and butternut squash. (See Chapter 12 for suggestions on preparing food for babies.)

Once it's clear that your baby has no adverse reaction to a food, it can be mixed with something he's had before – baby rice with fruit, for example, or parsnip and apple. Many babies will settle on two solid feeds a day for a while, taking milk for their other feeds. An example of a possible day's feeding for a baby of five or six months old is given below.

Suggested day's feeding for a five- or six-month-old baby

On waking   Milk feed.

10.00 a.m.   Baby rice with sieved banana. Sips of breast or
formula milk or cool, boiled water from an open
cup. Breast or bottle feed.

1.00 p.m.   Breast or bottle feed.

4.00 p.m.   Puréed carrots. Milk or water from an open cup.
Usual milk feed.

6.30 p.m.   Last breast or bottle feed.

This is an easy stage for parents, because it means you can be out
and about with your baby at lunch-time without having to bother
about food for him. Personally, I was in no hurry to move on to three
meals a day. But sure enough, just as my daughter, at the age of
four and a half months, had clearly insisted that she needed more
than milk, after a month or so she made it plain that her requirements now included a proper lunch.

My mother and I were sitting quietly, the baby playing happily
on a rug, when she suddenly began to fret anxiously. I listened for a
minute or two, thinking 'She can't be hungry, it's only two hours
since her mid-morning meal,' then found myself remarking 'She
sounds hungry.' 'She sounds hungry to me, too,' said my mother. So
up I got from my armchair, and three meals a day plus snacks it's
been ever since.

Drinking from a Cup

A baby can start learning to drink from an open cup from about
six months onwards. It's a good idea to give him sips from one at
mealtimes to encourage this skill. Protect him from spills, hold
him on your lap and hold a small cup up to his lips. As he mouths
it, tilt it so that a little runs into his mouth. He will probably be
startled and it may run straight out again. Give him a couple more
sips and then leave it. Try again in a day or two.

Many babies who have been introduced to a cup from an early

age can manage a two-handled plastic mug by the time they are eight or nine months old. Although there is a great range of lidded, spill-proof cups and beakers on the market, these are more useful for older babies and toddlers, especially when you're on the move. Drinking from an open cup is quite different from sucking from a teat or spout.

Unfortunately, not all babies are taught to drink from a cup at the age when they're most willing to learn. This may make them reluctant to use one later on, and cause them to cling to their bottles. If your baby starts having sips from an open cup soon after he starts on solid food, it helps make a clear distinction between drinking for thirst and eating for hunger.

Offer him cooled, boiled tap water, expressed breast milk or his usual formula milk. Mineral water can be high in minerals and salts, and is best avoided. Water is the perfect thirst-quencher, and your baby will drink it happily if he has it from the beginning. Give him water with meals, and as a regular drink to quench his thirst, especially in hot weather.

In addition to water, fruit juices (such as fresh orange juice), which contain Vitamin C, are a valuable extra as they aid the absorption of iron.

A Relaxed Approach

If you wait until your baby is ready, and introduce solid food gradually, allowing your baby to set the pace, you will be laying the foundations for a relaxed approach to food. Some babies make their likes and dislikes clear from the start; others eagerly gobble up anything you spoon their way. If your baby rejects one food, don't remark on it or try and persuade him to eat it. But offer it again in a few days – babies' preferences fluctuate wildly – and next time he may eat it quite happily.

One thing which often causes feeding problems is milk, especially milk in bottles. You may be at a loss as to why your baby rejects your lovingly prepared food, while overlooking the fact that he's consuming too much milk to have any appetite. Healthy babies do not need to be tempted to eat. They should be hungry enough to want to eat. If they're not, milk may well turn out to be the culprit.

74

• WEANING AND BOTTLES •

Weaning used to mean gradually phasing out the breast or bottle and replacing it with solid food, along with drinks from a cup. The baby moved from sucking his food to being spoon-fed and given sips from a cup, then to holding his spoon and cup himself. This marked definite steps in his development.

Weaning is also used to describe a switch from breast- to bottle-feeding. This can cause feeding problems when a baby who is well established on a mixed diet of solid food, say between nine months and a year, continues to have large quantities of milk in bottles as well. Unlimited bottles can interfere quite seriously with the shift to solid food and the feeding skills that go with it.

Remember that milk is a food, and a baby who is always full of milk isn't going to be hungry for anything else. Many early food difficulties have a simple explanation: the baby simply isn't hungry enough to want to eat what he is offered. Large quantities of milk can mean a baby is literally never hungry.

Sometimes, toddlers continue to be given full bottles of milk after meals, on the grounds that they haven't eaten much, and at least the milk will nourish them. Unfortunately, the bottles are usually a habit. The milk spoils the children's' appetites for their meals and gives them the idea that they needn't bother to eat at the table as they can always have a bottle of milk afterwards instead.

• NIGHT FEEDING •

No matter how little your baby eats during the day, avoid feeding him after bedtime beyond the first few months. Milk at night will make him less hungry for his meals, and prevent him developing a smooth rhythm of eating and sleeping.

Night feeding is the main cause of broken nights in babies under a year old. A good night's sleep, on the other hand, encourages good appetite and good temper. It helps your baby to manage his day and cope with new challenges – like eating. Night feeding interferes with both the nutritional and developmental benefits of solid food. A baby who drinks bottles of milk day and night may be undernourished without feeling hungry enough to eat.

There may be arguments over his poor appetite, instead of a glow of accomplishment as he learns to satisfy his own hunger. The whole issue of eating can become fraught with tension, and the comforting bottle of milk his escape from conflict over food. This impossible cycle can only be broken by cutting down his milk, especially at night.

Some people believe that whether a baby physically needs night feeding is irrelevant. If he wants it, they reason, even if it's for comfort not nutrition, then he needs it, and should have it. But prolonged night feeding is a learned habit. It doesn't do your baby any favours to encourage it. If you deliver all the comfort and reassurance your baby needs during the day, he is less likely to wake for it at night, and, when he does, it need not be accompanied by food. Babies are most settled and content when they sleep all night and wake eager for their breakfast, and naturally that makes your life easier and pleasanter too.

By the age of a year or so, other foods should have replaced milk as your baby's main source of nourishment. 'A pint a day' is often recommended as a rough guideline for toddlers, but if he's eating well and gaining weight there's no need to worry about his milk intake, and certainly no need to supply it in bottles. Milk on cereal, a drink of milk at breakfast and bedtime, and milk in the form of cheese and yoghurt add up to quite enough for a toddler who is eating a balanced and varied diet.

In general, it's a good idea to phase out bottles altogether at around the age of one year.

- The powerful sucking urge abates at about nine months and, from then on, many babies are excited enough by their new eating experiences not to miss the bottle.
- Too much milk will spoil an older baby's appetite for solid food, and may deprive him of essential nutrition.
- Developmentally, learning to feed himself is a big step forward for your baby, and encourages his progress in other areas as well. Bottles give him less reason to master these new skills.
- Your baby is more amenable at this age than he will be later on, when he will be more likely to resist change. An older toddler may resent it very much if you try to deprive him of his habitual bottle.

When she was nearly a year old, my baby was accustomed to a bedtime bottle of milk. Unsure whether she would be upset if I took it away, I put a colourful new beaker and the bottle side by side on the kitchen counter at bedtime and let her choose. She chose the new beaker, and never had another bottle. For me, it was yet another lesson in trusting my baby to know herself.

To sum up: rather than allowing your baby to move from the breast to unlimited bottles of milk in addition to meals, think of weaning as the gradual replacement of milk sucked from breast or bottle by solid food, supplemented with milk from a cup.

PLAN FOR INTRODUCING SOLID FOOD

► Leave the timing up to your baby. Most babies will make it clear they are no longer satisfied by milk alone at some time between four and six months.

► Let your baby experience the satisfaction of making his needs felt, and finding them met by you, rather than imposing solid food on him before he's ready.

► Choose a time when your baby is relaxed, cheerful and ready for a new experience.

► Offer baby rice for the first few days, mixed with breast milk, your baby's usual formula, or cooled, boiled water.

► Introduce new foods one at a time, leaving a few days between each one, so that you will know the cause of any adverse reaction. Begin teaching your baby to drink cooled, boiled water from an open cup from about six months.

► Once your baby is eating solids, try not to give him milk feeds after bedtime. Too much milk will spoil his appetite for his meals.

► Try and phase out bottles altogether by the age of about a year. This is much easier than it will be later on, and encourages your baby's appetite and sense of independence.

7

BABY FOOD
Good or Bad?

CHOOSING what to feed your baby should be simple, but because we have so much to choose from, it can become complicated. The more choice we have, the more our decisions get tangled up with feelings and attitudes about food, about babies, and about ourselves and the kind of parents we want to be.

For some women, cooking for their baby is part of being a good mother. When feeding represents caring, cooking is a way of expressing love and concern. It's a small step from here to the idea that a baby fed on ready-made, commercial baby food is somehow less loved. This is nonsense, of course, but it's a good example of how emotionally loaded feeding a baby can be.

Parents who don't feel this way about cooking may believe that commercial baby food is actually better for their baby, because it has been prepared by 'experts' under ideal conditions. Or they may prefer it for convenience, and consider it just as good as home-made food. Many, perhaps the majority, are short of time and rely heavily on commercial baby food, but deep down they believe their baby would be better off with home-cooked food, and perhaps that they themselves would be better parents if they took the time and trouble to cook for their baby.

• WHAT YOUR BABY REALLY NEEDS •

Being a good parent has nothing to do with how much time you spend cooking for your baby, or encouraging her to eat. Food that's ready in minutes takes the pressure off both of you, giving you more time for mothering, and more time for fun. Convenience is important, and the busier we are, the more important it is. Commercial baby food meets a genuine need, but it is parents' need for instant, portable meals, not babies' need for anything in particular which it contains.

Once we start to separate feeding from the emotional excess baggage that collects around it, we can see our babies' needs more clearly, distinct from our own conditioned responses and attitudes. In reality, very few of us are either full-blown earth mothers, contentedly shelling and sieving peas, or so busy that we can't mash a banana. Most of us want the same thing. We want to feed our babies as well as possible, but we can't spend half our lives in the kitchen in order to do it. In the time we do have, we may suspect that our babies would rather have a mother ready to play or chat than one chained to the cooker.

But baby-food manufacturers play on maternal guilt. Their advertising suggests that, if you only had time, you would grow your own vegetables and cook them with tender loving care, because nothing else is good enough for your baby. Having created this anxiety over an impossible ideal, they soothe it with assurances that they've done it all for you, and provided the perfect food for your baby on your behalf. Remember that advertising is designed to sell baby food. It bears little relation to what your baby actually needs.

So what does your baby really need? Food plays several different and important roles in your baby's life, as it does in everyone's.

Social Skills

Your baby learns to eat as part of learning about the world. In all cultures, eating has an important social dimension. People gather to eat, and join in family and community life. Eating with your baby plays a big part in this. So does learning about the kinds of food we eat, and how we share it.

If a baby is fed her own special food on her own, she's deprived of this social learning experience. She will be more enthusiastic when she's allowed to join in and eat the same food as those around her. Finger food gives her control over her own eating; being spoon-fed is a more passive, isolated experience. Examining her food and putting it in her mouth are good practice for being able to feed herself efficiently in due course. Bowls of baby food offer less scope for this.

Development

Eating solid food is one of the biggest spurs to development in the first year. It marks a great leap forward in your baby's dawning awareness of herself as a separate person, as well as in her competence and independence. Learning about different tastes is part of this experience.

When she had only milk, all her food tasted the same. Single foods, such as fruits or vegetables, have strong, fresh, clear tastes, which stimulate her developing palate. Commercial baby foods, on the whole, taste very much alike, and tend to be bland and sweet. If you don't know what it is, it's often difficult to detect the flavour of the main ingredient.

Elaborate mixtures, too, offer no advantages for a young baby just beginning to try new tastes. It is much more valuable for her to eat carrots while you say 'Carrots!' She will be learning what she's eating in a way that's impossible with a jar of mixed baby dinner. Enjoying or rejecting different foods also plays a role in the development of personality. If she refuses vegetable squash today, she may like it tomorrow, or prefer it mixed with potato. If she rejects a jar of mixed dinner, neither of you knows what she didn't like.

Nutrition

Her needs are very straightforward. At first, while milk remains her main source of nourishment, she simply needs more calories. Anything she eats will provide these, whether it's commercially prepared baby breakfast, plain baby rice or mashed banana. As her nutritional needs increase, milk gradually moves from centre stage into the background, becoming a valuable addition to a regime of three solid meals a day plus snacks. Her new requirements for protein, carbohydrates, fats, vitamins and minerals can easily be met by most ordinary foodstuffs, as well as by baby food.

Comparisons have shown that, gram for gram, the food values of commercial baby food match those of equivalent home-made dishes. A jar of baby dinner is as nourishing as a bit of grated cheese or minced chicken added to mashed carrots or potato. Nutritionally, a baby who is fed exclusively on commercial baby food will go short of nothing. The reason to limit its use is not because it doesn't meet your baby's nutritional needs. It is because it *also* provides a great deal your baby *doesn't* need.

• WHAT YOUR BABY DOESN'T NEED •

What your baby doesn't eat is as important as what she does. Most commercial baby meals are mixtures of several different foods. They also contain unnecessary added milk, starches and sugars. Although these may seem harmless, they can lead to a wide range of problems.

- A mixed diet, introduced too early, can trigger allergies. Complicated proteins also put too much strain on an immature digestive system. The previous chapter stressed the importance of introducing one new food at a time, so the cause of any reaction can be easily identified. Mixtures make this impossible.
- Overfeeding. Extra starches and sugars that your baby doesn't need for energy will be stored as fat. Infant obesity has been linked to health problems in adult life.
- A sweet tooth. If everything a baby eats tastes sweet, it's not surprising if she assumes that if it's food, it must be sweet, and refuses to eat anything that isn't. A baby may develop a sugar habit within a few months. This could lead to a lifelong craving for sweetness. The natural sugars in milk, fruit and vegetables are quite enough.
- Too much milk can interfere with your baby's transition to a good mixed diet. Since milk already forms a large part of her diet, and her cereal is also likely to be mixed with milk, adding dried milk to her food is pointless. This 'hidden' milk can make her milk intake too high for her to have much appetite for other food, and, as she gets older, she may go short of essential nutrients as a result.

The simple solution is to give your baby what she needs *and nothing else,* for as long as possible, and certainly until she is between nine months and a year old. The longer her diet is kept simple, the better, and home-prepared food makes this much easier.

• COMMERCIAL BABY FOODS •

Pull Apart that Label

As we browsed among the variety of baby food in my local super-market, a young couple with a baby a bit younger than mine said 'Hello'.

'We were just wondering,' said the father, 'if we should give him this. He's two and a half months old now, and it says 'from three months'.' He held out a packet labelled Sunshine Breakfast, or something similar.

'I wouldn't,' I replied. 'He's too young. Wait until he lets you know he needs more than milk, and then give him something plain and simple, like baby rice.'

'Oh,' said the father, indicating a picture of an orange on the box. 'We thought it would be good for him, with the orange juice.'

We chatted a bit more, then I went on my way, feeling oddly sad and angry. Those parents wanted to give their baby what was best for him, but their good intentions made them vulnerable. Although they knew good food when they saw it, their judgement had been swayed by a picture of an orange on a cardboard box. I don't blame them. We are surrounded by advertising, and manu-facturers have carefully constructed a link between buying something marketed for babies and caring for them.

If they had looked at the label on that box of cereal, those concerned parents would have discovered that orange juice barely featured. What it did contain a lot of, in common with most pack-aged baby cereals, was cornflour, dried milk and sugar. Cornflour produces a silky-smooth texture and bland taste. Milk makes it taste milky, and sugar makes it sweet. Your baby doesn't need any of this extra starch, milk and sugar, but bland, milky and sweet is what babies are supposed to like. In fact, it is what milk-fed babies like. But by the time a baby is ready for solids, his taste-buds (and his intelligence) are ready to be stimulated by a wider range of tastes and textures.

Before you buy baby food, look at the ingredients' label, rather than the name of the dish or the picture on the package. By law, ingredients must be listed in order of proportion, so that you can tell when there is more of one item than another. But there is no requirement to specify actual amounts, so there may be much more of one ingredient than the next on the list, or almost the same amount. There's no way of telling.

• If cornflour or modified starch is the second item, you may be feeding your baby nearly as much unnecessary starch as the main ingredient, which itself is often not what the name of the product leads you to expect.
• Next on the list may be dried milk. In addition to her usual milk and the milk used to mix cereals, this often adds up to more milk than your baby needs. This can contribute to overfeeding, or spoil your baby's appetite for other food. The whole idea of moving on to solids is to introduce foods other than milk into your baby's diet, not to increase her milk intake.
• Sugar usually features, often in more than one form. It may be listed as *glucose, maltose, maltodextrin, dextrose, sucrose, lactose, fructose, corn syrup, invert syrup* or *honey,* but it's all sugar. Sugar is pure carbohydrate and so can only be burned up as energy. Whatever exceeds your baby's immediate energy requirements will be broken down and stored as fat.

Here are some examples of typical added ingredients in popular baby foods:

'Toddler' ranges: 'Spaghetti Bolognese' included unnecessary extra starch in the form of cornflour. 'Vegetables and salmon' had skimmed milk as the third ingredient, before salmon, as well as wheatstarch and cornflour. 'Vegetable and chicken casserole' contained apples and apple juice (a source of sugar), cornflour and wheatstarch.

'From seven months' ranges: 'Tomato and cod' had skimmed milk as its fourth ingredient, before cod. Milk was the main ingredient in a cheese and vegetable bake. 'Cauliflower with lamb' had more skimmed milk than lamb. 'Carrots and chicken' was more water than chicken, and included milk, two kinds of cornflour and chicken fat. 'Pasta with chicken and mushrooms' had water as its first ingredient, as well as two kinds of cornflour and skimmed milk.

'**From four months' ranges:** 'Orange breakfast' contained three kinds of sugar – maltodextrin, sucrose and fructose. 'Fruit cereal' had sugar as its second ingredient, and two additional types of sugar for good measure. 'Oat cereal and apple' included two kinds of dried milk, two kinds of sugar and vegetable fat.

'Apple and banana cereal' contained apple juice (a source of sugar), and wheatstarch and cornflour, as well as rice flour. 'Creamed porridge' consisted of first milk, then water, cream, oats, sugar and cornflour, instead of simply milk (and/or water) and oats, as it would if you had made it yourself for a young baby. 'Yoghurt breakfast' included wheatstarch, cornflour and maize oil. 'Yoghurt and fruit breakfast' contained, in addition to yoghurt and fruit, three different sugars, three flours and three forms of milk.

A cereal designed for a baby's first taste of solids contained sugar and cornflour in addition to rice flour and two fruits, one of which was strawberry. Berries are not recommended for young babies, as they can trigger allergies. Apart from the unnecessary sugar and starch, if your baby reacted badly to the fruit, you wouldn't know which one to blame.

Among 'main courses' aimed at babies from four months old, 'vegetable hotpot' included sugar, skimmed milk, rice flour and added milk protein. 'Baked beans and bacon' had water as its main ingredient, as well as added cornflour and skimmed milk. A baby this young should not be having bacon at all. 'Vegetable and beef stew' listed tomatoes first (a food best saved for older babies, because it can trigger allergies). Sugar, starch and milk all came before beef.

Nutritionally, it's correct that a small baby should have very little meat. Ideally, she should have none at all until she is between six and nine months old. But the names of the meals are designed to make parents feel they are giving their baby a 'proper' dinner. To make it more suitable for young babies, the actual food inside is about as far removed from what an adult would expect from these dishes as it's possible to get.

Muesli is another example. In its original form, a chunky blend of oats, nuts and fruit, it's an excellent breakfast for adults and children, but unsuitable for young babies, who should not have nuts or high-fibre food. Adapted and marketed for babies from four months, however, and aimed at parents attracted to the idea of 'healthy' food for their infants, muesli is unrecognizable. One packet contained, in addition to oats, maltodextrin (a sugar), skimmed-milk powder, vegetable fat and wheatflour.

The trend for marketing baby food with adult appeal reaches absurd heights with packets labelled 'from four months' claiming to contain international dishes in baby form, such as 'Chinese noodles', 'Southern fried chicken', and 'pizza'. What is the point of buying exotic mixtures for a baby who has only just begun to venture into solid food? She doesn't need her palate titillated by unusual flavours. Plain carrots are a great novelty to her. Anyway, there's nothing new about the food inside these packets, which includes the usual added starches and sugars.

Chocolate pudding aimed at babies from four months old is equally wrong-headed. Children demand chocolate soon enough, even if they are never offered it at home. Why deliberately create a taste for chocolate in a small baby?

Baby Food: The Drawbacks

Commercial baby food has two major disadvantages: it tends to have too many ingredients and it includes too much of what your baby doesn't need. There is also is its sameness. Home-prepared food varies from day to day, in taste and texture. Commercial baby food doesn't.

The dozens of ingredients in commercial baby food offer a kind of fake variety, with no real benefits to your baby. Even the most limited range of home-made food varies in a way that gives your baby genuine new information and experiences. Different textures become important as your baby grows. If she's used to smooth purées, or the uniform chopped texture of baby food designed for older babies, she may be put off by unfamiliar variations in real food when she is expected to eat it.

Your baby is much less likely to be a fussy eater if she is accustomed early on to a wide variety of tastes. Babies, in fact, enjoy quite strong flavours, if they are given a chance to try them. Fresh puréed vegetables taste quite different from puréed vegetables with added cornflour, milk and sugar. If you want your child to eat vegetables, it's not much good springing them on her for the first time as a toddler, by which time her opinions and preferences are quite strong. A stalk of broccoli, for example, could be an unpleasant shock if most of what you've had before tastes of milk and sugar. On the other hand, babies allowed to experiment have shown a fondness for strong tastes, such as those of garlic, aubergine, cauliflower – and broccoli.

Above all, learning to feed herself is one of the most exciting and developmentally beneficial things she will do in her first year. This is much easier to do if she has finger food. The longer you go on spooning purées into her mouth, the more likely she is to resist. Alternatively, she may become so accustomed to being fed that she refuses to feed herself when you decide she should.

A child who is given control over her own eating has a powerful incentive. Finger food is much less messy, but if you can't bear the mess when she wields a spoon herself, let her do it at suppertime, just before her bath, and spread newspaper under the high-chair.

Allowing your baby to select her own food from what's available gives much greater flexibility, and helps your baby meet her own nutritional needs more exactly. Babies and small children are very good at balancing their own diets if given the chance. My own child goes on an orange binge when fighting off a cold, as if something tells her she needs extra Vitamin C. A baby on a growth spurt may eat a whole potato for lunch three days running, then restrict herself to a single Brussels sprout on day four. Baby food rules out this valuable process of self-selection. Your baby can have more main course (if there's any in the jar), or more pudding, but it's impossible to have a bit more of any one item.

Better Baby Food

When I was weaning my daughter three years ago, the enormous choice of baby food in the local supermarket didn't include plain baby rice. Rice cereal with strawberries, yes; with bananas, yes; on its own, no. I had to track it down in the pharmacist's. Today, in response to growing demand, there is a larger range of pure, simple and organic baby foods than ever before. Nutritionally, these are better for your baby, because they contain no added milk, sugar or starches. 'Pasta and vegetables' is likely to consist of just pasta and vegetables, which lets you control what goes into your baby.

Organic mixed dinners are ideal to have on stand-by, for travelling or emergencies. So are jars and tins of single vegetables and fruits with no added ingredients, now much more widely available. These are good on their own for young babies, or mixed with other food when you're in a hurry – baby rice and puréed apple, for example. They're useful when you want a small quantity of one fruit or vegetable.

But even the purest, simplest baby food won't make the best exclusive diet, because it suffers from the same uniformity of taste and texture as all manufactured food. It also does nothing to introduce your baby to family meals. On top of that, baby food is expensive, and the better the quality, the more expensive. Without cheap, starchy fillers, organic baby food costs much more than other products.

• THE SIMPLE SOLUTION •

The simple solution is the one that's easy for you, cheap, *and* best for your baby. Easy means instant, or as close to it as possible. Cheap means good value, knowing what you're paying for, and not throwing money away. And best for your baby means food that offers her nutritional, social and developmental advantages.

There is undoubted satisfaction in providing your baby's food yourself, watching her take pleasure in it, and gradually handing over control of her eating. But if you haven't time to prepare meals, or don't enjoy cooking, jars may seem the only answer. There is another way.

It's perfectly possible to have all the benefits of home-prepared food without sacrificing the convenience of a jar. The simple solution is to make sure that home-made food is also fast food.

If you keep it simple, there's no need to buy food or drink especially marketed for babies and children. It's surprisingly easy to provide your baby with everything she needs, and nothing she doesn't, without buying anything special, except perhaps baby rice at first. It's worth remembering that leaflets on weaning are sponsored by baby-food manufacturers. It is not in their interests to point out that a sandwich would nourish your baby just as well as a jar of complicated dinner.

One secret is to realize that 'home-made' doesn't have to mean cooked. Plenty of foods, just plonked on a plate, provide all the nutrition of a cooked dinner. Short cuts mean you never have to spend more than a few minutes getting your baby's dinner unless you feel like it. It may be quick, easy and convenient for you, but it also introduces your baby to real food, provides optimum nutrition and leads her naturally to good eating patterns. Home-made fast food is the subject of the next chapter.

FEEDING PLAN FOR USING BABY FOOD

▶ Learning about food and eating is one of the biggest events of your baby's first year. Choose food that will give her optimum nutrition, while also providing a social-eating experience and stimulating her development.

▶ If food for your baby is quick, easy and convenient for you, so much the better. That doesn't mean it has to come from packets and jars.

▶ Read the labels on baby food. Try to avoid giving your baby added milk, sugar and starches.

▶ Organic ranges and jars of single fruits and vegetables with no added ingredients are best.

▶ The younger your baby, the more important it is to keep her diet as simple as possible. Aim to give her everything she needs and nothing she doesn't.

▶ Solid food should, over the second half of the first year, gradually replace milk as your baby's main source of nourishment. Make sure she isn't taking so much 'hidden' milk that it spoils her appetite for other food.

▶ Your baby's tastes are in the process of being formed, and they're shaped by what you give her to eat and drink. What you choose to feed your baby in her first year will be a major influence on her later habits and health.

8

MEALS, SNACKS, DRINKS AND TREATS

BUYING a minimum from the baby-food shelves makes it much easier to keep your baby's diet simple. It gives you the flexibility to respond to his needs as he has them. It's better not to be too well prepared for weaning to solids. Let the idea come from your baby. Focus, instead, on developing communication, to make it easy for him to tell you how he feels. Look at him, listen to him, before deciding what he needs.

One father tells a story about being on holiday with his young baby, who one fine day suddenly seemed discontent, no matter how often he was breast-fed. They had stopped their car in the middle of rural France, trying to soothe their baby, when it occurred to the father that food might be the answer. Hunting through their supplies and provisions, he came up with a garlic press and a banana. He pushed the banana through the garlic press and offered it to the baby, who ate it gratefully and never looked back. That is a truly baby-led approach to weaning. There's no reason why it should be any more complicated than that.

· SNACKS ARE IMPORTANT ·

Over the second half of the first year, solid food gradually replaces milk as your baby's main source of nourishment. But the *number* of feeds he will need remains the same. Remembering this is a key to the simple solution.

- If you expect your baby to need regular snacks as well as his meals, you can be prepared by carrying healthy titbits and a drink around with you.
- You don't need to go into a shop if your baby demands something

to eat or drink. This means he won't be tempted by colourful displays of sweets and crisps when he's hungry.

- Providing regular healthy snacks between meals prevents low blood-sugar levels and the behaviour problems they cause.
- A snack or drink, produced from your pocket or bag at the right moment, can instantly soothe and distract a restless baby.
- Properly timed snacks mean your baby won't become ravenous and demand food just before meals.

Many people consider eating between meals a bad thing. It is, when it means constant snacking or eating large quantities. This will spoil a child's appetite for meals. If it doesn't, it will cause overfeeding. His diet is much less likely to be healthy if spur-of-the-moment snacks take the place of regular, balanced meals.

Snacks have an important place in your baby's diet, but that doesn't mean he should eat what he pleases, when he pleases. It means expecting him to need food in addition to his three meals, and including it in his regular diet. A toddler is not 'eating between meals' if his mid-morning juice and breadstick is, itself, a snack meal – just a smaller one, perhaps taken in the park or push-chair.

Some adults find it easy to stick to three meals a day and nothing else, but many people, especially if their regular meals are low in protein, find they need something in between. Babies and children, who have high energy requirements and small stomachs, nearly always do.

Providing them with regular energy boosts in the form of healthy snacks also helps conserve protein for growth and body-building. Protein will be broken down to supply energy needs if these are not immediately met. This process uses up yet more energy. Often, a toddler demanding sweets or biscuits is just plain hungry. A piece of bread will do just as well.

Suggestions for nutritious, portable and instant snacks can be found in Chapter 12.

• MILK AND MEALS •

Some authorities say milk should not be given between meals, as it stays in the stomach and reduces the appetite for meals. Milk should be seen as a food, rather than a drink. If a milk feed (or a milky drink in a cup) is treated as a proper snack between meals, it meets a real nutritional need and helps to sustain blood-sugar levels. What will interfere with meals is *too much* milk.

Night feeding is a prime culprit. A baby old enough for solids is old enough to sleep through the night. After this age, night feeding becomes a habit, and will prevent healthy rhythms of eating and sleeping. During the day, give your baby some of his milk in a cup. Give him his bottles in your arms, so you can see when he's had enough. Don't let him have full bottles of milk to carry around and swig on constantly. That's like eating all the time, and it's no better for him than it is for us.

When your baby first starts solids, his meals are no more than an addition to his usual regime of five or six milk feeds a day. When he moves on to three meals a day, he will still need two or three milk feeds in between, although they will be smaller as solid food meets more of his nutritional needs, and he won't concentrate on them as he used to. Given the chance, he will naturally reduce the total amount of milk he takes as his solid intake increases.

A breast-fed baby will tend to stop feeding vigorously as soon as he's satisfied. A bottle-fed baby is more at risk of overfeeding on milk. He may suck for pleasure, or out of habit, and take in more than he needs. This will interfere with his progress to a full mixed diet of solid food. Introducing an open cup helps here, as the effort of mastering this new skill will mean that your baby will drink only as much as he needs to.

For years, we've been told that babies must have a minimum of a pint of milk a day. This 'magic pint' is badly misunderstood. Its purpose is to provide a sort of guarantee: as long as a baby has roughly this much milk as well as his meals, however little he eats, he will not starve. It certainly should not mean that a lusty toddler who eats a balanced diet, including dairy products like yoghurt, butter, cheese and ice-cream, should empty a pint bottle of milk every day as well.

Trust your baby to regulate his own intake. Lack of interest in meals by young babies may be a sign that they are not ready for solids. Among older babies, it's often caused by too much milk. Appetites are frequently transformed when night-time feeds, or frequent daytime bottles, are cut out.

• MEALS AND SNACKS •

A baby of a year or so might have a cup of milk before his morning nap, and maybe some water with apple or orange juice in it during the afternoon, accompanied by a breadstick, or a piece of bread and butter. He will probably have a beaker or bottle of milk before bed. Together with his three meals, this gives him the same number of feeds as he had on milk alone. It adds up to the traditional five meals of breakfast, elevenses, lunch, tea, supper, plus a milky drink at bedtime.

If both meals and snacks are nutritious, how much he decides to eat at each meal is less important. Everything he eats will help him grow and maintain a stable metabolism. There will be days when he wants no afternoon snack, or barely touches his morning milk. That's as it should be, as he regulates his intake to suit his changing needs. If you offer him five or six meals and snacks a day (remembering a drink of milk is a snack), he can eat as he needs to. You won't need to provide 'empty' calories in the form of sugary, fatty snacks when he's hungry or thirsty at odd times of the day.

• FIRST MEALS: PURE AND INSTANT •

Banana is a perfect early food, needing only to be sieved or mashed. Another, less commonly used, is avocado pear. This is a traditional weaning food in countries where it grows. Like banana, it's delicious as well as highly nutritious. It's much cheaper than it used to be, and widely available.

Fruits and vegetables become instant meals if you have a freezer and a microwave, both of which really come into their own when feeding babies and children. Freezing purées in ice-cube trays and storing the cubes in the freezer means a home-cooked meal can be defrosted in a minute. Chapter 12 gives directions for making frozen cubes of fruit and vegetable purées.

This system allows you to spend a total of half an hour a week preparing two or three different meals for your baby for the week ahead. It also means someone else can give your baby instant home-cooked food, and provides portable baby food. You can take a frozen cube in a small plastic container when you go out, and it will defrost naturally in time for the next meal.

Mixed and alternated with banana and avocado, cereal and, occasionally, vegetables that you have cooked for yourself and pushed through a sieve, these instant home-made cubes provide all the variety and nutrition you need for the first couple of months on solids.

Unless you enjoy cooking especially for your baby, there's no need to do it once you've made a supply of cubes, and no need to buy baby food either. Rice cereal, followed by oats, bread and other grains from six months or so (once you're sure he can tolerate gluten), plus fruit and vegetables, will provide everything that your baby needs in addition to milk until he's about nine months old. Keep it simple: there's nothing wrong with banana every day.

Stop feeding your baby as soon as he indicates that he's had enough, or you will sow the seeds of resistance to food. Don't worry at all about how much or how little he eats. Remember that milk remains his main food for some time. The transition to a full mixed diet happens later. At this stage, it's much more important that he enjoys his early feeding experiences.

• SIX TO NINE MONTHS: THE GREAT • FINGER FOOD ADVENTURE

When your baby starts sitting up and grabbing the spoon, he can experiment with feeding himself. Even when the food lands on his nose or ear, it's good practice. A spoon each is one solution: he smears cereal on his face, you spoon it into his mouth. A bread-stick to dip into mashed vegetables or fruit is fun and nutrition combined. Fine purées are no longer necessary – mashed with a fork is fine. The really, exciting breakthrough of this stage, the answer to life from now on, is finger food.

- It's less messy.
- Small pieces have lots of baby appeal. His curiosity makes him want to pick them up, and the natural next step is to put them into his mouth.
- It's easier than loading and aiming a spoon.
- Successful self-feeding gives your baby confidence and a sense of achievement.
- Many nutritious, tasty finger foods need little or no cooking.

● It liberates you from spoon-feeding duty.

After a few weeks, a baby who has had the chance to practise will be quite efficient at picking up food and putting it into his mouth, and will be very pleased with himself. Many babies who are allowed to feed themselves as soon as they want to, and are given plenty of finger food, are independent feeders by the age of a year or so. Always keep a close eye on your baby, to make sure he doesn't choke.

With a high-chair, finger foods really come into their own. Spread an array of bite-sized morsels on the tray at mealtimes, and let him experiment to his heart's content. (See Chapter 12 for suggestions.) Gradually, these can become a more substantial part of his meal. Once he's good at eating with his fingers, there's no need to provide a bowl of something as well. A sandwich and some fruit is a nutritious meal. You'll know when he's eating efficiently enough to satisfy his own appetite – he'll show you.

Bread

Bread is the perfect finger food. Bread should be soft brown, whole-meal or nutritious white, such as an organic loaf. Babies should not have over-refined white bread, or granary-style wholewheat, which is too rough and high in fibre.

Luckily, most babies love bread. Toast soldiers and sandwiches open up a whole new world of easy and enjoyable eating. It's fun for your baby to share cinnamon toast with his family, or mouth a bit of bread in a café. Chapter 12 contains ideas for sandwiches and other instant, nutritious meals and snacks for your baby or toddler.

The next chapter contains guidelines on when to introduce wheat and other grains containing gluten, which can trigger an allergic reaction in sensitive babies.

Teething

Once he starts teething, your baby will be glad of something to gnaw. Baby rusks, marketed as both weaning food and handy snack, are a bad buy. They're soft, sticky and unbelievably messy, and even the reduced-sugar varieties are high in sugar. Basically, it's an expensive way of giving your baby a sweet biscuit.

Give him an oatcake or a rice-cake instead. Bickie Pegs™ are hard, dry little sticks, like ship's biscuits, sold especially for teething babies. These are good at odd times of the day, as they're satisfying to bite and suck but don't provide food. Crusts are also popular. So are sticks of raw carrot and cucumber.

Dairy Products

Dairy products contain lots of protein, calcium and vitamins to meet increased nutritional needs. Live yoghurt contains bacteria that help keep the digestive system healthy, as well as lactase, an enzyme that helps digest milk. Butter is high in Vitamins A and D, and provides energy in a concentrated form appropriate for your baby's rapid growth. Give him a finger of buttered toast while you get his breakfast and he'll be getting nutrition as well as eating practice.

Cottage cheese on bread or toast is another winner. It's a mild-tasting, high-protein food that's also light and easily digestible. Ricotta is a soft, smooth cheese which mixes well with fruit. Mild, hard cheese, such as Edam or Cheddar, is good grated on mashed vegetables or pasta.

The next chapter discusses when various foods, including cow's milk and other dairy products, can be safely introduced.

Adapting to Changes

Many babies have a growth and development spurt around now, and this is obvious in their eating patterns. A six-month-old may eat very much like a five-month-old for a while, then at seven or eight months suddenly seem to go up a gear and eat twice as much, twice as eagerly. One day he'll pick at slices of banana, the next he'll grab the banana and eat it whole. Be guided by his appetite and growth rate rather than his age.

A hungrier baby may appreciate a pudding course. When you introduce one, don't make it a sugary dessert. Give him fruit, raw or cooked, perhaps mixed with plain, full-cream yoghurt.

Once he's been on three meals a day for a while, there'll be more of a distinction between them. He can have what older children have for breakfast – bread or toast, cereal and fruit. A baby's cereal should be fine-textured and unsugared. Instant oatmeal is a good choice. Ordinary porridge takes five minutes to cook. It's highly nutritious, cheap, and children love it. Babies can manage porridge from about eight months.

For convenience, you may choose either lunch or tea/supper to be his 'main' meal. Traditionally, this is usually cooked. While that may suit you, remember a cooked meal isn't any more nutritious than an uncooked one. A cheese sandwich and an apple is an instant meal that provides everything your baby needs. There's no rule that says he must have meat and two vegetables.

• FROM NINE MONTHS •

From now on, your baby will start to benefit from the high-quality protein in meat and fish. Finely chop a little to add to his vegetables. Chicken is ideal. Give him a few shreds to pick up in his fingers. Babies also enjoy gnawing on a chicken bone, but be careful to strip it of all small bones and gristle before you give it to him. Fish is high in protein, light and easily digestible. White, non-oily fish is an excellent meal for babies. Liver is a rich source of iron. Chapter 12 contains fast-food recipes and suggestions for using meat, chicken and fish.

Peanut butter is an instant source of high-quality protein. A piece of bread and peanut butter makes a nutritious meal. See Chapter 9 for guidelines on including peanuts in the diet of babies who may be prone to allergies.

Acidic fruits, such as tomatoes and oranges, should cause no digestive difficulties from this age. The juice of an orange in water makes a nutritious and refreshing drink.

Vegetarian Babies

If you plan to feed your baby a vegetarian diet, you will need to make sure that his sources of protein and iron are adequate. Protein is supplied by dairy products, pulses and grains (such as baked beans on toast), and, later, eggs. (See Chapter 9 for guidelines on when to introduce eggs.) In Western society, too much protein is more of a problem for most people than too little. Iron-rich food includes spinach, lentils, chick peas, soya-bean curd, brown rice, almonds, cashew nuts, dates, dried peaches and apricots.

•EATING PATTERNS•

Sample of an eating pattern in the first year

Four-and-a-half months	Demands solid food. Solids once a day, one new food every few days: Baby rice, banana, apple, pear, carrots, avocado pear. Then mixtures of these.

Five months

On waking	Breast feed.
Mid-morning	Sieved banana and baby rice, followed by breast feed.
Lunch	Breast feed.
Tea-time	Fruit (frozen cube of puréed cooked apple or pear, or ripe, sieved pear) and baby rice. Breast feed.
Bedtime	Breast feed.

Six-and-a-half months

On waking	Breast feed.
Breakfast	Mashed banana, or cube of puréed apple or pear, or mashed, ripe raw pear, with baby rice and usual milk.
Before morning nap	Breast feed.
Lunch	Mashed vegetables, for example, squash and carrot. Cube of fruit purée.
Mid-afternoon	Breast feed if wanted. Otherwise, practise drinking milk from a cup. Sometimes a finger of toast, or an oatcake.
Supper	Mashed vegetables, for example, parsnip and potato.
Bedtime	Breast feed.

Seven months	Eating much more.
On waking	Breast feed.
Breakfast	Fingers of toast. Mashed fruit and/or oat cereal. Milk from cup.
Before morning nap	Breast feed.
Lunch	Mashed mixed vegetables. Yoghurt and puréed fruit,
Mid-afternoon	Milk from cup, breast or bottle.
Supper	Avocado sandwich. Rice pudding or mashed banana.
Bedtime	Breast feed.

Eight months	
On waking	Breast feed.
Breakfast	As before, but less eager for food. Will now drop bread over side of high-chair and watch where it goes rather than eat it. Can feed self and use mug, very messily.
Before morning nap	Breast feed.
Lunch	Vegetable stew, frozen in small portions, sometimes with added grated cheese. Greek yoghurt with home-frozen apple purée.
Mid-afternoon	Milk from cup, breast or bottle.
Supper	Fruit and ricotta cheese with bread and butter, or pasta with grated cheese and butter.
Bedtime	Breast or bottle feed.

Ten months	
On waking	Forgetting to ask for the breast. More interested in crawling.
Breakfast	Peanut butter on bread, in addition to fruit and cereal.

Mid-morning	Milk in cup.
Lunch	Chopped chicken or flaked fish, with cubes of potato and carrot, or broccoli or cauliflower florets.
Mid-afternoon	Water with orange or apple juice in it. Sometimes squares of bread and peanut butter, or an oatcake.
Supper	Pasta with ready-made sieved tomato (passata) and grated cheese. Tangerine.
Bedtime	Milk in bottle.

One year

Breakfast	Whole milk in cup. Oatmeal and banana. Toast and butter.
Before morning nap	Milk in cup.
Lunch	Fish-finger, broccoli florets. Sometimes bread and butter too. Tangerine. Or roast chicken and roast potato cut up small, with gravy and cubes of cooked carrot. Ice-cream, or yoghurt and fruit.
Mid-afternoon	Water with apple or orange juice. Breadstick or raisins.
Supper	Scrambled egg, bread and butter. Half a pear.
Bedtime	Drink of milk from beaker.

| **All meals** | Water offered from an open cup at all meals. Sips first offered and taken at five and a half months. Plastic mug placed on high-chair tray for independent drinking (with tactful assistance!) from eight months. |

This is an example of the typical eating habits of just one baby, whose mother happened to record them at the time. Naturally, every baby will arrive at his own pattern, and vary in his needs, preferences, and appetite. The sample clearly shows the rapid progress that takes place over six months or so, from the first taste of solids to self-feeding and joining in family meals.

Notice that finger foods, introduced at six months, quickly become a large part of this baby's diet. By the age of a year, much of his food can be eaten with his fingers. This eases the frustrations of learning to use a spoon efficiently.

It's also clear from this sample that what a baby eats at the age of one year can be the foundation of a suitable diet for several years. The major differences will be increased quantity (although this will vary from day to day, and week to week, as he adjusts his intake to his changing needs) and added new elements, as he explores a wider variety of foods. But this is a healthy and well-balanced basic eating pattern for a pre-schooler, as well as a one-year-old.

• DRINKS •

The Importance of Water

Water is the best possible thirst-quencher. If your baby learns to drink water when he's thirsty, he won't overload his system with the sugar in fruit juice, soft drinks and milk. Remember that milk is a food and beverage combined. If your baby drinks milk when he's thirsty, this can contribute to overfeeding, or spoil his appetite for other food.

Plain tap water should be boiled, cooled and stored in a sterilized container until your baby is approaching six months old, when his immune system is well developed. After that, tap water is fine. Don't use mineral water, which contains too many salts and minerals for babies. If you need to use bottled water, choose the brand lowest in salt (the sodium figure should be less than 25mg per litre), and boil it first.

Exclusively breast-fed babies do not usually need water, unless they're refusing the breast, or feverish. Breast milk varies from feed to feed, to suit your baby's needs. Infant formula doesn't, so bottle-fed babies should be offered water from the start. Once your baby is on solids, he needs water. From about six months, he can start to practise taking sips of water from an open cup. This kills two birds with one stone: he learns an important skill, and he learns that water relieves his thirst.

A toddler should generally have plain water with meals, and it should always be available between meals. When you go out with your child, pack a beaker of water. Your baby will quickly learn to ask for it when he's thirsty.

Fruit Juice and Other Drinks

You can buy special bottled water for babies. This is expensive, and unnecessary. Boiled tap water in a sterilized container is just as good. Don't buy bottled water with fruit flavourings. The whole idea is to get your baby accustomed to drinking plain water. If he never tastes it, he won't get the habit. The same applies to fruit juices and cordials manufactured for babies.

These are promoted for their vitamin content, but there are plenty of vitamins in fruit and vegetables. Vitamin drops, although not essential for healthy babies who eat a wide variety of fresh food, are a better idea than fruit juices and cordials, because they don't come with a dose of sugar. Sugar-free drinks contain artificial sweeteners. There's no need for your baby to consume sugar or chemical sweeteners when he's thirsty.

For variety, an older baby will enjoy diluted fruit juice. This should be just a splash of fruit juice in water, providing a fruity taste with the minimum of sugar. Again, read the label on fruit juice to see what you're getting. If it's called fruit 'drink', rather than 'juice', it may contain more sugar than fruit.

From nine months or so, the juice of an orange diluted with water is nutritious and refreshing. Most toddlers enjoy blackcurrant cordial, which should be heavily diluted – a splash of syrup to a cup of water. On the whole, don't give fruit juice or cordials more than once a day, and always with food, bearing in mind that fruit juice aids the absorption of iron. Between meals, diluted fruit juice, along with an oatcake or breadstick, makes a good snack.

Some mothers think their children can't be expected to drink water if they don't drink it themselves. Babies and children are great mimics, it's true, and it does help to set an example. But the key is what your baby is used to drinking himself. Many toddlers dislike fizzy drinks if they are unfamiliar with them.

Fizzy drinks, including diet drinks and even carbonated water, should be avoided for as long as possible. All fizzy drinks contain acid, which erodes tooth enamel. Dentists say the consumption of fizzy drinks by children now poses a more serious problem than tooth decay from too many sweets.

Of course, toddlers are soon offered boxed fruit juices and fizzy drinks at birthday parties and other children's houses. Occasionally, it does no harm, and making a fuss will only make forbidden fruit more desirable. But make it clear that these things are just for special treats, and never offer fizzy drinks to your baby yourself.

Babies and children should never have coffee, tea or alcohol. Tannin in tea prevents the absorption of iron. Caffeine, found in both coffee and tea, is addictive. So is alcohol. There is nothing amusing about giving a baby sips of alcohol from an adult's glass. His immature liver should not have to cope with toxic substances.

• SWEETS, CHOCOLATES AND FIZZY • DRINKS: SHOULD THEY BE BANNED?

Sweets and fizzy drinks do most harm when they're consumed on their own. So the best time for sugary treats is with meals. Ice-cream or jelly, for instance, are ideal special-occasion puddings for toddlers and children. A biscuit could be served with plain yoghurt for tea. A gift of chocolate could be saved for after lunch.

It's worth considering a total ban on sweets, chocolates and fizzy drinks for the under-twos. This saves you having to think about it, and helps you be consistent. It has real benefits for your child's health, and prevents the development of a sweet tooth. Babies under two years old are not difficult to steer away from these things. It's older toddlers and children who may come to look on sweets as a right.

A baby is easily distracted, and tact and sleight of hand can make sweets disappear without him noticing. It does require vigilance, though, as it won't work once he has possession. It also helps to explain in advance to grandparents, friends and relations. If someone gives you sweets for your baby, thank them warmly and put the sweets away when no-one is looking. The less of an issue it is, the better. If your child does have some sweets, don't react.

There comes a time when such close vigilance is inappropriate. Once he can hold his own at a birthday tea, it's unfair and interfering to hover over his shoulder and whip food away. Now's the time to accept that parties include sweet treats. But keep them for special occasions. If your child hankers after chocolates in a shop, don't react crossly and tell him they're bad for him. Agree, in a matter-of-fact way, that they look pretty, but laugh off the idea that you might buy them, as you might if he admired a sports car in a showroom window.

A child who feels he is being unreasonably deprived is the one who is going to make the most fuss. So give him lots of positive attention and non-food treats, and make sure he knows whining is never rewarded. With a first child, you can explain that certain things are not for children. When there are other children around, it's harder. But a baby is not a child, and he can wait until he is at least two years old to join in children's treats.

Adapt treats for your baby so that they're more healthy, but still delicious. Hot chocolate can be made with half milk, half hot water, and half a teaspoon of drinking chocolate. To a two-year-old who doesn't know what hot chocolate is supposed to taste like, the whole idea is thrilling. Keep the treat factor high and the sugar element low.

Since most children enjoy sweets and fizzy drinks, you may feel that banning them for babies is a lost cause, if not mean. This is not so. The longer a child is kept away from soft drinks and sweets, which contain no nutritional element at all, the better for his health. And the longer you keep your child's diet simple and healthy, the more likely he is to regulate it in that direction himself when he has free choice. For the few years that you control what your child eats and drinks, you may as well use your influence for good.

PLAN FOR MEALS, SNACKS, DRINKS AND TREATS

▶ Plan for your baby to have three meals and two snacks a day, perhaps with a bedtime drink of milk as well.
▶ Regular healthy snacks help to maintain high blood-sugar levels, providing sustained energy and good humour.
▶ Remember that a drink of milk is a snack meal. Too much milk

can prevent your child making the transition to a good mixed diet of solid food.

▶ Let your baby regulate his own intake of food and drink. Be guided by his appetite and growth rate rather than his age.

▶ Help him learn to drink from a cup from about six months onwards, as bottles can contribute to overfeeding.

▶ Offer water regularly to a baby who has started solids, and to bottle-fed babies from the start. It's never too soon for your baby to get into the habit of drinking water when he's thirsty. Provide water with meals, and carry a beaker of water when you're out and about.

▶ Any fruit juices or fruit cordials should be given extremely diluted, only with food, and from a cup.

▶ Offer your baby hard, unsugared snacks to gnaw when he's teething, such as crusts, Bickie Pegs™ and carrot sticks, rather than baby rusks or biscuits.

▶ Optimum nutrition need not mean a cooked meal. A cheese sandwich and fruit is just as good.

▶ Sugar should be avoided as far as possible. It has no nutritional value, damages teeth, spoils the appetite for meals and contributes to health problems.

▶ Sweets do most harm when eaten on their own, so try and save any sugary treats for after meals.

▶ Consider the benefits of a total ban on chocolate, sweets and fizzy drinks for babies under two years old. If you do this, don't make an issue of it.

9

WHAT, WHEN, WHY
Allergy and Immunity

WHAT BABIES should be given to eat, and when, is a complicated question. Ask for suggestions about feeding your baby, or pick up a book or leaflet on the subject, and you'll be given detailed and often contradictory advice. Young babies, we're told, can have rice but not wheat, bananas but not strawberries, spinach but not tomatoes, fish but not eggs. Not only is the advice confusing, it keeps changing, too. New foods are constantly being added to the 'avoid' list.

For many parents, the solution is to opt out of the whole tricky business. It can seem as if you need a degree in nutrition to get it right. Baby-food manufacturers employ nutritionists to make sure that their products are suitable for babies, so you may conclude that commercial baby food is better, and safer, than home-prepared food. Manufacturers are naturally eager to encourage the idea that they are the true experts in feeding your baby.

In fact, feeding a baby should be very simple indeed. A young baby's diet should, ideally, consist of far fewer foodstuffs than the mixtures that make up most baby food. Overfeeding, especially of protein, is one of the main causes of feeding problems. Using ready-made baby food can encourage this. Baby 'dinners', including meat or fish and vegetables, are designed to be followed by a separate pudding. This may be what many adults consider a good diet, but it is altogether too much for young babies.

Nothing that you feed a young baby is insignificant. While her digestive and immune systems are immature, it is worth considering carefully what you put into them. Official guidelines on when to introduce different foods are mostly intended to minimize the risk of triggering any allergic reaction. Some are a precaution against infection.

The advice has to be broad, as it's meant for all babies, whatever their individual characteristics and circumstances. This means it must err on the side of caution. Although the majority of children are not predisposed to allergies, feeding advice is tailored to the few that are. Guidelines that will reduce the risk of allergic reaction in sensitive individuals are likely to be unnecessarily strict for babies who have no family history of allergy.

Once you understand the reasons for delaying the introduction of certain foods, you can make up your own mind what's most important to you. Certainly, there's no reason why feeding guidelines should make feeding appear difficult, encourage you to believe baby-food manufacturers know best, or put you off giving your baby home-prepared food.

• ALLERGY •

The incidence of childhood allergies has increased considerably in recent years. There are several reasons for this, including the increased complexity of our diet, and the practice of giving solid food to very young babies. An allergy develops when a baby is sensitized by something in her diet, or her environment, before her immune system is developed enough to cope with it. A predisposition to allergy is inherited, so your baby is likely to be particularly sensitive if there's a family history of allergies.

Most children are not predisposed to allergies, and will not develop them. Nevertheless, it makes sense to protect your young baby's immature digestive system from unnecessary stress. An adverse reaction doesn't always show up immediately. Frequently, the system is sensitized over time by exposure to something, and this eventually triggers an allergic reaction.

The best precaution is to keep your baby's diet as simple as possible, for as long as possible. If the variety of food she's given is kept to a bare minimum in the first month or so of solids, her digestive system will have a chance to develop before tackling more complex food. You will also make your own life easy, as offering just a few basic meals means no worrying about what your baby should or shouldn't have.

Infant Formula and Allergy

One of the ways in which a new-born baby's digestive system is immature is that the bowel may still be slightly porous. Complex proteins can leak through the gut and enter the blood, where they may be rejected as foreign bodies. It can take some time for this to happen, as the immature immune system may not react at first. When it does, it will start producing antibodies. When sufficient antibodies have been produced, the next time the protein is introduced into the system, it will react. Typical allergic reactions include rashes, vomiting, diarrhoea, constipation, colic and failure to thrive.

Infant formula milk is modified cow's milk. It is constantly being adapted to make it as close to breast milk as possible, but the basic cow's milk protein, casein, cannot be changed. It is this protein which can sensitize a young baby's immature gut and produce an adverse reaction, which is diagnosed as *cow's milk protein allergy*. Sometimes a soya formula is prescribed instead. However, soya protein has also been known to trigger allergic reactions in sensitive infants. Breast milk is best for babies who are allergic to cow's milk.

Cow's milk protein allergy, which is sometimes triggered when a baby is weaned from breast to bottle at a very young age, is sometimes mistakenly called *lactose intolerance*. Lactose intolerance occurs when the enzyme lactase, which digests milk sugars, is missing from the digestive system. This is usually a temporary condition, which sometimes follows gastro-enteritis. Milk sugar, called *lactose*, is present in all milks, including breast milk, so affected babies have to be fed on a soya formula. Yoghurt, which includes the enzyme lactase, is sometimes tolerated.

A marked rise in the number of children with a potentially fatal peanut allergy has caused concern over the past year or so. Swelling and breathing difficulties occur immediately after eating even minute quantities of peanuts, and sufferers may die after repeated exposure. Many people with peanut allergy also have other allergic illnesses, such as asthma, eczema and rhinitis, or hayfever, as well as a family history of allergy.

Various theories have been put forward to explain why peanut allergy is increasing with each generation, now being found in children as young as one or two years old. One suggestion is that sensitive babies are given peanut butter too early. Another is that traces of peanut may be passed from mother to baby during breast-feeding, or even in the womb. The role of peanut oil in infant formula is currently being investigated.

Whether currently popular brands of infant formula contain peanut oil is impossible to tell from the labels, as ingredients present in less than a certain quantity do not have to be listed. Fish oil, however, does appear on the list of ingredients of at least one well-known brand of infant formula. The younger the baby, and the more immature the immune system, the greater the risk that complex proteins will trigger a reaction in a sensitive individual.

Allergy, and its relationship to immunity, is an area of rapidly expanding knowledge. We know much more about it than we did ten or twenty years ago, and new information is becoming available all the time. Common sense suggests that links between substances such as fish oil and peanut oil in infant formula and allergic reactions in young children will be a subject for continuing research.

It's already known that full breast-feeding for the first months of life offers optimal protection against later allergic reactions. Ideally, babies with a family history of allergy should have nothing but breast milk for six months.

• IMMUNITY •

A strong immune system is vital for health. Good resistance to infection is a valuable asset, one that you can help your child to develop, and one that will stand her in good stead throughout adult life.

When your baby is born, her immune system is underdeveloped, making her extremely vulnerable to infection. The development of her immune system is influenced by her early care and feeding, as well as by heredity. What you choose to feed your baby makes a big difference to her capacity to resist infection and fight disease.

The sooner her immune system becomes strong, the greater the benefit to her health. Every time we succumb to an infection, it puts a strain on our bodies and lowers resistance, which is why another infection so often follows. Equally, each time the body successfully fights off infection, its resistance becomes stronger. At its simplest, a child who has never been ill is less likely to succumb to infection.

Breast Milk and Immunity

The first fluid produced by the breasts, colostrum, is very high in antibodies. This helps protect your new-born baby from infection. Colostrum lasts until your milk comes in, somewhere between the third and fifth day. It is all the food that a new-born baby needs. The importance of colostrum is one of the reasons why early breast-feeding, even for one week, is so beneficial to your baby.

Your own antibodies, the resistance acquired during your lifetime's exposure to infection, are passed to your baby in your breast milk. This continues for as long as you breast-feed, so even if you eventually cut breast-feeding down to one or two feeds a day, you will still be giving your baby's immune system a boost.

The part played by breast-feeding in building immunity is so valuable that it is worth breast-feeding for this reason alone, even if you're not persuaded by discussion of its nutritional and emotional benefits.

• SUGAR AND SALT •
Why is Sugar a Bad Thing?

- Natural sugars occur in most food, especially fruit, vegetables and milk. These supply quite enough for our energy needs. Extra sugar has no nutritional value, and can cause behaviour problems, obesity and tooth decay.
- When a baby sucks fruit juice from a bottle or beaker, or a toddler sucks on a lollipop, their mouths are bathed in sugar. Few things do more harm to their developing teeth.
- Sugar is quickly transformed into energy. Too much can make your child manic and hyperactive, then cause energy levels to slump when her blood-sugar level falls. This creates a craving for more sugar, producing a vicious circle.
- Excess sugar over-stimulates the pancreas to produce insulin. This is thought to be a factor in the development of diabetes.
- Sugar can contribute to underfeeding. Sugary snacks and drinks take away the appetite for other food, and your child may go short of essential nutrients.
- Excess sugar can cause overfeeding if a child has too many sweet snacks and drinks on top of his regular meals.

Why is Salt a Bad Thing?

- Salt puts a strain on a young baby's kidneys, and can cause dehydration. Young babies are not able to excrete salt efficiently, and too much makes it difficult to maintain the correct balance of fluid levels.
- Just as too many sweet things create a sweet tooth, salty food is habit-forming.
- A taste for salt, continued into childhood and adulthood, can contribute to high blood pressure and heart problems.

Don't add salt to your baby's food. When cooking for the family, remove the baby's portions before seasoning. If she's always had her food without salt, she won't miss it, and she'll learn to appreciate more subtle flavours.

• A PRACTICAL GUIDE •

The simple solution to coping with changing guidelines on infant feeding is to introduce new foods into your baby's diet as slowly as possible. The younger she is, the simpler her diet should be. The older she gets, the greater the variety of food she will be able to appreciate and digest efficiently.

In practice, this has a natural logic that helps to make your life easy. For the first few weeks of solids, while your baby is learning about food and eating, you can provide a very limited selection of food. Milk will still provide almost all her nutritional needs, apart from a few extra calories.

Gradually, as your baby takes an interest in feeding herself, becoming able to munch with her gums and handle finger foods, the range of everyday foods she can share becomes larger, and your role as spoon-feeder correspondingly smaller. By the end of her first year, she can eat what you do, appropriately served, and naturally with certain exceptions, such as very spicy food, which might upset her digestion.

The following guide to the first year shows how simple feeding a baby can be.

A guide to feeding in the first year

Four to six months

Usual milk, plus, if more food is wanted, baby rice, bananas, apples, pears and carrots, on their own at first, then combined as you like.

Delay solids until six months for infants with a family history of allergies.

Additional suitable foods for those who want to offer them: avocado pear, potato, sweet potato, parsnips, butternut squash.

NOTE All food needs to be puréed or finely mashed.

Six to nine months

All vegetables and fruits, with the exception of tomatoes, citrus fruits and berries, which may be too acidic for some babies and can trigger allergies in sensitive individuals.

Add: Pulses, such as baked beans, lentils, peas and beans.

Why not before? Can be difficult for young babies to digest.

Add: Bread.

Why not before? Wheat contains gluten, which is one of the more common causes of allergy. Gluten sensitivity is a factor in a rare and sometimes serious illness, coeliac disease.

Add: Oats, rye and barley.

Why not before? They also contain gluten.

Add: Pasta.

Why not before? Pasta is made from wheat, which contains gluten.

Add: Single-ingredient oils, such as sunflower oil and olive oil.

Why not before? They put an unnecessary strain on the immature digestive system.

Add: Dairy products. Babies who are fed on formula milk, and are therefore accustomed to cow's milk protein, can now have dairy products such as butter, cheese, yoghurt and ice-cream. Breast-fed babies are better off not having them for a bit longer.

Why not before? Dairy products are one of the more common causes of allergic reactions.

Add: Eggs, thoroughly cooked.

Why not before? Eggs are a favourite early food, and high in iron and protein, but, because of the presence of salmonella bacteria in some poultry flocks, eggs are now regarded as a high-risk food. However, if you are perfectly confident about your source of eggs, they can be given cooked in the usual ways.

NOTE Food can be mashed instead of puréed. As much as possible should be offered as finger food. Raw fruit and vegetables should be given whole, or in pieces big enough for your baby to hold and gnaw without the risk of choking.

Nine to twelve months

Add: Meat, liver, chicken and fish.

Why not before? Animal proteins can trigger allergies if they are introduced earlier, and the concentrated protein they provide is not necessary for younger babies. However, babies not prone to allergies may be given these foods earlier.

Add: Tomatoes, citrus fruit and berries.

Why not before? Acidic foods can be difficult to digest and sometimes trigger allergic reactions.

Add: Peanut butter, unless there is a tendency to allergy. Whole nuts should always be avoided, because of the risk of choking.

Why not before? Peanuts can trigger a serious allergic reaction in sensitive individuals.

Add: Dairy products, if not introduced earlier. If there is any tendency to allergy, this should be delayed until one year.

Why not before? Dairy products are one of the more common causes of allergic reactions.

Milk: Official guidelines are that babies should not have cow's milk as a regular drink before the age of one year, although it can be used in cooking. It's recommended that babies remain on breast milk, or formula milk, which is fortified with iron, until then.

Why not before? Cow's milk is low in iron. However, if your baby is eating a good mixed diet including sources of iron (for example, red meat, pulses, green leafy vegetables, dried fruit), pasteurized whole cow's milk is suitable, unless there is a tendency to allergy.

NOTE Food can be of many different textures: chopped, roughly mashed and whole, as finger food.

One year onwards

Add: Dairy products, if not introduced earlier.

Add: Whole cow's milk as a drink, if not introduced earlier.

Add: Processed foods, such as pâté, salami and cooked meats, if you want your child to have them.

Why not before? These products are high in phosphates, so should be eaten only occasionally and in small amounts. The risk of pre-cooked food being contaminated by bacteria, including listeria, is the reason to delay its introduction until the immune system is strong. Do not give unpasteurized milk or cheese.

NOTE Family meals can be served cut up small. Fingers are still much easier for your baby to use efficiently than a spoon or fork. Being able to feed herself is more important than manners at this age.

If your baby has these basic foods, both separately and combined in everyday dishes, such as sandwiches, pasta, salads, soups and casseroles, and nothing else in her first year, she will have a balanced, healthy diet with optimal nutrition, and the risk of triggering allergy or digestive problems will have been reduced to a minimum.

The examples above are not intended as a prescription. Naturally, there's no rule that says your baby must have apples or pears, and everyone will have favourite foods which aren't listed, but which may well be perfectly suitable for your baby. The guide is simply to show how easy and straightforward feeding a baby can be.

The sample feeding programme also highlights a second important point: the period when you need to take special care with your baby's diet is very short. Her system is most vulnerable when she's very young, under six months old.

It's no coincidence that babies are about six months old when they begin to chew with their gums, sit up, and grasp things and convey them to their mouths. These developments equip them to manage solid food in a way they couldn't before. If the introduction of solids is delayed until your baby makes it clear that she's ready, she will be close to an age when her digestive system can cope with a much wider range of food, and you will be able to be more relaxed about what she eats.

She will also be much closer to being able to feed herself at least part of her meals. The era of fine purées, baby rice, tiny tastes and dedicated spoon-feeding need only be a few weeks long.

FEEDING PLAN FOR WHAT, WHEN AND WHY

▶ Your baby's diet should be kept as simple as possible, for as long as possible. Overfeeding, especially of protein, is one of the main causes of feeding problems. The early introduction of solids can trigger allergies and digestive difficulties.

▶ A young baby's digestive and immune systems are immature and vulnerable. Everything that goes into her should be carefully considered.

▶ The simple solution is to limit food for babies under six months to a bare minimum. The younger your baby, the simpler her diet should be. The older she gets, the greater the variety of food she will be able to appreciate and digest efficiently.

▶ Sugar and salt should both be kept to a minimum.

▶ Breast milk offers optimal protection against both infection and allergic reactions in young babies.

▶ A predisposition to allergy is inherited. Babies with a family history of allergies should ideally be fed only breast milk for the first six months. The introduction of foods known to trigger allergies, such as wheat and dairy products, should be delayed.

▶ Once you know the reasons for feeding guidelines, you can make up your own mind which are important to you. Most are designed to reduce the risk of triggering allergies. Some are a precaution against infection.

▶ What you choose to feed your baby makes a big difference to her capacity to resist infection and fight disease.

10

CONFLICT OVER FOOD

WHEN I was first pregnant, a friend who has two daughters warned me that food struggles would soon loom large in my life. I said I refused to get worked up about it.

'You wait,' she said. 'You wait until you've bought and mixed the best organic cereals, made sure you've got fresh, creamy milk, and lovingly presented your toddler with a delicious, nutritious breakfast. Then watch her push it away, whining "Don'wannit". I challenge you not to get upset.'

'I won't,' I said. 'For a start, I wouldn't go to that much trouble in the first place. You're just setting yourself up.' Then I began to wonder. Did this happen to everyone? Would it happen to me?

'No,' said my mother. 'You won't change when you become a mother. You'll do things your way.'

She was right. I never did get worked up about food. Plenty of other things, yes, but not food. To my mind, eating should be an enjoyable experience, and conflict over meals ruins any chance of that. What matters to me is a pleasant atmosphere, not how much anyone eats or doesn't eat.

My friend's description of the effort and frustration involved in feeding her toddler goes to the heart of many mothers' anxiety about feeding. Worry that a child isn't eating enough, or not enough of the right kind of food, makes you tense. Your child picks up the tension and refuses food, either because he can't relax or simply to enjoy his power to get his mother dancing attendance.

That's why a child will often eat better away from home, when his relationship with his mother is taken out of the picture. Fretting when a child eats less than you expect is counter-productive. It amounts to a general rule: the more you worry about how little he eats, the less he's likely to eat.

Of course, it's natural to be concerned that your child should eat well. The best way to achieve this is to put suitable food in front of him and let him get on with it. It helps to make a deliberate policy decision not to worry about how much he eats unless he's losing weight or appears unwell. A small appetite, by itself, is not a sign of anything wrong.

• DOING TOO MUCH •

Feeding is very closely tied up with mothering, and mothers tend to judge themselves by how well their baby eats. Because of this, you can try too hard to feed your child. This puts him off, so you try even harder, creating a vicious cycle. The simple solution is to refuse to get into arguments about food. Remember it takes two to have a battle. Don't join in, and there can be no conflict.

The best way to deal with a feeding problem is never to develop one in the first place. Trusting your child to know his own needs, and letting him eat what he wants in his own way, is the key to successful, pleasant mealtimes.

Of course, allowing him to eat what he wants doesn't mean providing treats on demand. It means allowing your baby to select from the food you offer him. If everything you offer him is nutritious and what you want him to eat, it doesn't much matter whether he eats some or all of it, and in what proportions. You choose the food; he decides how much to eat.

Babies and children love to be allowed to choose. With so little control over their lives, small decisions provide a gratifying sense of power. So give your child as many appropriate choices as you can. Appropriate choices are ones where it makes no difference to you what he decides. 'Would you like peas or broccoli?' 'An apple or a tangerine?' Being given choices like this satisfies a child's need for control, and he's less likely to refuse food which he's chosen himself. Rejecting food is often a child's way of rebelling against his mother's controlling influence over him.

• KEEPING THE PRESSURE OFF •

Pressure on a child to eat comes in many forms. Healthy babies who are gaining weight are routinely urged to finish their bottles or take just a bit more. This is pressure. So is starting a baby on solids before he's ready. A baby who is distressed and bewildered by his first experience of food has not had the best introduction to eating. From when you first start feeding your baby, remember to stop as soon as he indicates that he's had enough. Resist the temptation to persuade him to have one more spoonful. There's no point in giving him more food than he needs. If he won't take it, it starts an unhealthy cycle of pressure and resistance. If he will, it may cause overfeeding.

Large helpings of food overwhelm a small person, and may take away his appetite altogether. Tiny portions are much more appealing. If your baby wants more, he will make it plain, and both of you will be pleased: you because he is eating well, he because you understood and responded to his request. Communication, as well as appetite, has been enhanced. You have also spared yourself the sight of a plateful of uneaten food.

Be sure to allow plenty of time, more than you think it could possibly take to eat such a small quantity of food. Too often, babies and toddlers are hurried and scolded over their food, not allowed to feed themselves, and urged to empty their plates. All this sows the seeds of resentment, and the natural way for a baby to express feelings of being bullied over food is by refusing to eat.

Lucy's first case as a health visitor was a challenging one. An eleven-month-old baby, his parents' fifth child, had been admitted to hospital because he was losing weight. 'I went to see the family at home for a check-up, assuming the hospital would have solved the problem,' recalls Lucy. 'I was horrified by what I saw. He looked like a baby starving in an African famine. His arms and legs were stick-thin, his eyes weeping, his skin papery and dry. He had lost weight since being discharged from hospital. His parents said he ate nothing, but was still breast-feeding. The hospital doctor hadn't been able to find out what was wrong.'

'I visited the family once a week, but every enquiry drew a blank. I kept saying: "Let him eat what he wants, whenever he's hungry. Don't feed him, let him feed himself. Let him eat socially with his brothers and sisters." I still had no idea what was going

117

on. But as the weeks went by, he slowly started to gain weight.'

'Then I didn't see the family for three weeks and the baby lost weight again. Next, the father went abroad for a long time on family business. Then the baby really started putting on weight. Two months later, the mother finally told me that the father had become very angry when the baby first refused to eat and had force-fed him. After that, the baby had refused to eat anything at all.'

Parents are often reminded that a healthy baby won't starve himself into illness. The one exception, as this story shows, is when he is force-fed. Although force-feeding is a rare form of abuse, this shocking example does serve to illustrate how badly a baby will react against pressure on him to eat.

At the other extreme, games like pretending the spoon is an aeroplane flying food into his mouth, or 'One for mummy, one for daddy,' although they're fun ways to persuade a baby or toddler to eat a bit more, are also a subtle form of pressure. They interfere with his own control over his eating. They also send him a clear message that how much he eats matters very much to the adults around him. This is the last idea you want to give him.

Watching mummy jumping through hoops to persuade him to eat gives him a sense of power, and it's more entertaining than eating his lunch. On the other hand, if mummy sits there calmly chatting, he will turn his pursuit of power elsewhere – probably to attempting mastery of his food. A baby who is scolded, bullied, urged and cajoled is certainly not going to eat any better than one who is let alone, and he's much more likely to become a problem eater.

It's a good idea, once the early stage of introducing solids has passed, to deliberately think up ways to let your baby eat in peace, while still keeping a close eye on him. Having someone hover over his every mouthful is as irritating for him as it would be for an adult. It's also irritating for you to watch him messing with his food. The temptation to interfere and take over is strong. So leave him to it, and turn a blind eye to the whole business.

Washing up, turning round frequently for eye contact, smiles and chat, is a good tactic. So is sitting companionably with him, casually looking through your mail or half-reading a magazine or newspaper, perhaps commenting on it to your child.

Describe his food in a positive but matter-of-fact way, and praise him for eating independently, but chat to him about other things as well, such as your plans for the rest of the day – anything that takes the whole focus of your attention off his eating habits, and allows you to relate to him in a friendly, relaxed way. Appear to ignore his eating as far as you can. This makes him more likely to take an interest in his food.

When he stops eating, leave the plate in front of him a few minutes longer. Babies and children often decide they'll have a bit more if the choice is left up to them. A baby playing with his food may be exploring before eating it, but messing around once eating has stopped is usually a sign that he has had enough. Take his plate away without critical comment.

If he has finger food, it's easy to provide enough variety for him to take what he likes. But if he has a single dish and takes one mouthful and no more, you may suspect he doesn't like the taste. You could offer him a piece of bread and butter or cheese instead. Don't assume he won't eat the dish next time you serve it, and don't tell him (or anyone else in earshot) that he doesn't like it. If there's a pudding course, give it to him as usual. All these tactics will prevent him developing a negative attitude towards food and meals in the future.

For many small children, the word 'No' is like a red rag to a bull. So try and say it as little as possible, however often you mean it. When your toddler asks for a biscuit, you could say: 'Yes! We'll have one after lunch.' Even 'There are no more biscuits in the tin,' or 'We never have biscuits before breakfast' is more interesting than a flat 'No', which he's liable to take personally.

Always try and sit down with your baby or child for at least part of his meal, and ideally eat something yourself, even if it's just a piece of toast or fruit. This has lots of benefits:

● It keeps you occupied and less likely to interfere with his eating.
● It encourages him to eat as he tries to copy you.
● It helps you relax.
● It gives your baby a sense of shared mealtimes as pleasant social events.

• THE IMPORTANCE OF SELF-FEEDING •

As far as possible, from as early as possible, let your baby eat, rather than feeding him. From the beginning, think of his eating as his business, not yours. It's your job to provide nutritious food, but what he eats, and how much of it, is his.

Spoon-feeding is an uncomfortably passive experience, as anyone who has experienced it knows. Hand over control to your baby as soon as he shows interest. Let him grab the spoon and experiment with feeding himself. As soon as he can aim bits of food at his mouth, finger food can become a major part of his diet. Feeding himself gives him a tremendous sense of independence, and his natural curiosity will move him to try whatever morsels he finds on his high-chair tray.

Alice vividly demonstrated the link between self-feeding and overall development. Aged fifteen months, she was still being spoon fed. She didn't join in family meals because she fussed and resisted. Trying to get a few spoonsful into her was an ordeal. Meanwhile, her friend of the same age sat at the table and ate the same food as everyone else.

One morning, on a shared family holiday, after Alice had spent an hour refusing to eat her cereal and her friend had used a dinner fork to polish off two farm eggs, Alice's father had an idea. 'Let's stop feeding her baby food,' he said. 'If her friend can feed herself, so can Alice.'

Alice was transformed. Not only did she take to finger foods with enthusiasm, she walked for the first time next day, and slept better at night. Her protests had not really been about eating, but about what and how she was fed. Basically, she was angry about being treated like a baby.

Food is an arena where all sorts of other struggles are conducted, and these conflicts and misunderstandings are at the root of most eating problems. The more you can defuse the whole issue of eating by letting your baby take charge of his own feeding, the less opportunity there is for food to become a battleground between you.

• 'DON'T LIKE IT' •

Some babies eagerly swallow everything you spoon into them. Others have definite preferences from the start. Either way, avoid introducing the idea of likes and dislikes yourself. Let that come from your child in his own time. If he doesn't eat something, don't tell him that he doesn't like it. Babies are great mimics, so it's worth making an effort not to say in front of him that you don't like a certain food yourself.

If each meal offers some variety, a child can decide not to eat his tomato today without missing out on nutrition. He may very well eat it tomorrow. Next time it's on the menu, give it to him without comment.

Often, if a food has been rejected once, parents don't offer it again. Then it's not surprising if the number of foods which a child will eat becomes limited. Food should be an interesting and enjoyable adventure. If you don't want to encourage fussy eating, it's best to ignore quirks.

Some parents enjoy discovering their child's likes and dislikes, compiling quite a list by the end of the first year, and talking about it to the child and to others. This makes no sense if you want your child to eat a wide variety of food, as it encourages him to take a sort of perverse pride in what he won't eat.

As your baby gets older, he'll discover the power of complaint. He'll say 'Don't like it', even if he's never heard the words from you. Don't argue. Just say 'Well, eat the carrots then,' or something similar, and carry on as usual.

One little girl of two years old, always fussy about tastes, took to whining 'Don't like it' as soon as her plate was placed before her, no matter what was on it. Faced with this, you can only reasonably point out that she can't know she doesn't like it until she's tried it, and leave it at that. Don't get drawn into a discussion. If she sees everyone else eating happily, she'll probably try some if she can do it without having to back down in a battle of wills. Children don't like to lose face. If you don't make it an issue, it won't be a matter of pride to stick to their guns.

• STEP BACK AND RELAX •

No parent sets out to confront their child over food. On the contrary, parents want a quiet life. It's toddlers who are entertained by a confrontation. They don't mind when it ends the meal, as they probably weren't hungry anyway. It can be hard for loving parents to accept that their child enjoys provoking them into anger, but remember small children like being the centre of attention. If it consists of praise and smiles, good; but scolding and badgering is better than nothing.

That's why almost any reaction to provocative behaviour can cause it to escalate. To your toddler, it's all grist to his mill. As far as possible, ignore behaviour you don't like, including not eating as you think he should.

In Chapter 1, we saw how conflict over food arises when parents don't realize their child is biologically destined to be small, especially when he has been a big baby. A child who is growing slowly may eat much less than his parents expect, but it will be enough for his needs. Sometimes this only becomes clear when the child reaches school age and is clearly among the smallest children in his class. Equally, another child may eat 'well' simply because he is programmed to be tall, and needs plenty of food to fuel his rapid growth. This is not a virtue, just a biological fact.

Patterns of growth also play a part. Babies have evident growth spurts, when they suddenly demand more milk than before, and so do toddlers and small children. This is one of the reasons why small children's appetites fluctuate so widely, and why it makes sense to let them regulate their own intake. A small child may grow so slowly that he never has a big appetite. A tall child may be on a permanent growth spurt, with a voracious appetite to match. Most children grow in fits and starts, and their appetites vary accordingly.

Babies' and children's energy requirements differ not only from individual to individual, but from one stage of development to another, and from day to day. A child who is fighting off an infection which you are not aware of may eat more, or less, for a day or two. Fatigue may cause a meal to be refused.

Babies usually need less food after about six months, until crawling ushers in another surge in energy requirements. After the age of one year, when the most rapid growth in the child's life is over, he may need less fuel than before. That's why it's toddlers who are most often regarded as 'problem' eaters.

The best policy is to look at what your child eats over a week, rather than meal by meal, or day by day. If you adopt a definite policy of not worrying until you can see a whole week's pattern, the 'problem' usually disappears by itself. At the end of a week, either the child will have changed tack or you will have forgotten to worry about it – frequently both.

Whatever you do, a relaxed attitude is your greatest ally. Keeping detailed charts of exactly what your child eats is sometimes recommended, as a way of reassuring yourself that he isn't actually starving. Doing this for a week won't hurt, if it will reduce your anxiety. But in general the whole idea is to be less preoccupied with what your child eats, not more.

• 'JUST ONE BITE' •

What do you do when your child refuses to touch his dinner altogether? First of all, don't take it personally. He is not rejecting your cooking, or your mothering, or you. He just doesn't feel like eating his lunch.

As to how to manage the situation, there are several schools of thought. Some parents put the food away and bring it out again at the next meal. That's fine if it's not done as punishment or to make a point. If the child simply wasn't hungry at lunch, he may well eat the same food at supper. But if the food is brought out to teach him a lesson, he'll resent it and refuse it again.

Other families have a rule that children must have one mouthful of everything on their plate before they can have the next course or end the meal. I favoured this approach myself until a friend and I faced a mutiny by three small girls over a cauliflower cheese. Thrilled with their solidarity, not one of them would take a single bite. Since you can't make a child eat, a rule you can't enforce isn't much use. On the other hand, one episode like this need not undo the general principle of trying before you decide.

The ultimate laid-back approach is to go along with it and allow your child to eat nothing until the next meal or snack. This is probably best, if you have the strength for it. A toddler usually only needs to try an experiment like this once or twice before deciding not to make it a way of life. But if he wants nothing because he's not hungry, then he wants nothing, and should not be offered an alternative, or a biscuit in an hour's time because he's had no lunch. Otherwise he'll learn that refusing food is the way to manipulate you into giving him something he prefers.

If your child does go on a hunger-strike and appears otherwise healthy and normal, keep your nerve. As long as he drinks water, he'll be fine for up to a week, which is much longer than most children go without eating anything at all. Remember milk is food. Most hunger-strikers usually take milk, and often nibble here and there as well.

At two and a half years old, faced with the combination of a long journey, a tummy bug, and post-Christmas burn-out, my daughter refused all meals for six days. She drank milk, and she ate bits of bread now and then. It wore me down, even though I knew she wouldn't starve. Sure enough, on day seven, she ate a whole bowl of cereal at breakfast and never looked back.

Poking around in your child's food, sorting it into 'must eat' and 'may leave' piles, or bribing him with promises of pudding or sweets if he eats his carrots, is getting too involved. You want to convey the message that food is for eating, not for bargaining over.

• FOOD AND DISCIPLINE •

Food and discipline are easily confused, because there are so many social conventions around behaviour at mealtimes. When considering what's reasonable, ask yourself what we expect of adults. You would not insist guests clear their plates, but you would object if they threw them on the floor. You wouldn't refuse them pudding if they didn't eat their salad, but you might ask them to leave if they screamed that the salad was disgusting.

In general, eating is not a matter for discipline, while behaviour is. Sometimes, a child gets into a state at mealtimes because he's frantic with hunger. His blood-sugar levels are so low he can't cope any more. Many adults suffer a version of the same thing, becoming irritable or exhausted when hungry.

It's annoying to have to deal with an hysterical child when you know he'll be fine as soon as he gets some food inside him. But being impatient or angry and pressing him to eat will only make matters worse. He needs to calm down before he will feel like eating.

That might mean letting the tantrum run its course, sitting quietly with him until he recovers. Put his food on the table and let him decide when he's ready to eat it. Eating your own food may encourage him to copy you.

Meals are well suited to the 'time-out' approach. An out-of-control or noisily defiant child can be removed from the room and asked to come back as soon as he's ready to eat his lunch. This gives him a chance to cool down without feeling humiliated, or becoming the centre of attention. He may not always be able to manage himself, but, underneath, he wants to enjoy his meals as much as you do. Give him a chance to achieve that without a fight.

Always be on the look-out for ways to defuse conflict. He will make you angry at times, but it takes two to have a row. Once the storm has passed, try and find a way to soothe your own ruffled feathers, even if it's only taking a few deep breaths, looking out of the window, or concentrating on something other than your child for a short while. Bottling up your own feelings produces tension, resentment and flare-ups.

The Pudding Problem

Having refused most or all of his lunch, a toddler will see no inconsistency in demanding pudding. This is only a problem if his usual pudding is a sweet treat, rather than a nutritious part of his meal. Naturally, you don't want him to have a sugary dessert and nothing else. But if pudding is routinely fruit, perhaps with plain yoghurt, it's just as good for him as the rejected main course, and will supply the missing nutrition too. (See Chapter 12 for suggestions.)

Happily producing his healthy pudding, however much or little he has eaten, has the advantage of making you appear cooperative and friendly, and encouraging similar behaviour in your child. It also avoids the trap of making a sharp distinction between different foods. You don't want to reinforce the notion that pudding is a treasure but lasagne a trial.

For the same reason, when there is a special pudding, it's probably wise to allow your toddler his share, however little he's eaten before. A treat should be a treat; there's no point in turning it into a bone of contention. But treats are yours to offer, not his right to demand whenever he wants.

'He'll Only Eat Pizza'

This is unheard of in societies where food is scarce. Fad diets are impossible without the cooperation of adults because, if they didn't provide pizza, the child would eventually eat something else rather than starve to death. On the whole, fads won't develop if a wide variety of food is routinely offered, and if the elements of the diet are kept as simple as possible.

Not paying too much attention to a child's likes and dislikes also helps. Often, fads are inadvertently created by loving parents who are pleased to find something their child eats with enthusiasm. He is given it often. Soon, he demands it all the time. Interestingly, there don't seem to be any children who will eat only eat spinach, or cauliflower. This suggests that fad diets are a weapon a child uses to make his parents give him the food he fancies.

A faddy eater is using food to wield power over his parents. Every toddler needs to do this, but the natural impulse to test his parents can, and should, be steered away from the business of eating. If he demands a particular food, agree calmly that it's delicious, but add that 'We don't have it every day'. If he protests, let him protest. Don't get involved in a fight, and don't give in. Just keep producing his food as usual and, sooner or later, he'll eat.

On the other hand, make sure that the food you do give him is appealing. Offer his preferred foods regularly, so he doesn't feel deprived, but make them part of a varied diet. A child who has pizza, chips, hamburgers and chocolate sometimes is not going to become an addict. It's his everyday habits that count.

Another approach is to go along with the fad, while reassuring yourself, by consulting nutritional tables if necessary, that he's getting what he needs to preserve his health. It's true that all phases pass in time. The drawback of allowing fad diets, though, is that it gives the child too much power over what happens in the household. He needs to learn where the limits are, and making up rules about what food is provided should be beyond the scope of his authority.

• FAT BABIES AND OVERFEEDING •

Far more parents worry that their babies and children eat too little than that they eat too much. However, in affluent societies like ours, overfeeding is more common than underfeeding. It's not unusual for parents to complain 'My child never eats', when close observation will reveal that, in fact, he never stops eating.

'Grazing', as it's known, and eating problems often go hand in hand. It's hardly surprising if a child eats nothing at meals if he regularly has chocolates, sweets, crisps, sweetened yoghurts, ice-creams, lollies and sugary drinks in between. In babies under a year old, overfeeding is likely to take the form of too much milk, as discussed in Chapter 8.

Overfeeding produces extra fat stores which may become the foundation of a lifelong weight problem. Although fat babies were once regarded as bonny, we now know that obesity is not healthy in infancy, childhood or adulthood, and it's best avoided from the start. A baby can be considered too fat if his weight is out of proportion to his height on his growth chart.

Feeding your baby skimmed milk and other low-fat products is not the answer, as we saw in Chapter 1. Babies have small stomachs, and they need concentrated nutrition to fuel their rapid growth. Instead, make sure you don't feed your baby more than he wants to eat. Be sensitive to his signals that he has had enough. Some eager-to-please babies will start eating again after they have finished if they see that's what you want them to do.

The simple way to make sure your baby doesn't get fat is to let him control how much he eats. If you give him nutritious food, and let him stop as soon as he has enough, his appetite will naturally regulate his intake.

FEEDING PLAN FOR AVOIDING CONFLICT OVER FOOD

▶ Try and keep tension out of your feeding relationship with your child. Make meals relaxed and friendly.

▶ The more you worry about how much he eats, the less he's likely to eat.

▶ Don't put pressure on your child to eat. That means not urging a baby to finish his bottle, not starting solids before your baby is ready, giving small helpings, allowing plenty of time, and being sure to stop as soon as your child indicates he's had enough.

► Provide a variety of suitable food and trust your child to regulate his own intake according to his needs. You choose the food; let him decide how much to eat.

► Allow your child to make his own simple choices, such as which fruit to take from the bowl. He's more likely to eat food he's chosen himself. Constructively encourage his desire for independence and control.

► Let your child feed himself as soon as he shows interest. His food is your business; his eating should be his own.

► Keep eating separate from discipline. Don't fight over food. If he's out of control, let him leave the room until he's able to calm down.

► While still keeping a close eye on him, allow your child to eat in peace. Keep the focus off his eating, or not eating.

► Don't make an issue of likes and dislikes, his or yours. Offer a wide variety of food without making sharp distinctions between different foods.

► Never get into an argument over whether or not your child is entitled to pudding. Side-step the issue by making pudding a nutritious part of his meal. That way, it can follow the main course or replace it.

► Don't use food as a bribe, punishment or reward.

11
TWELVE GOLDEN RULES

THE SIMPLE solution is to feed your baby whatever is easy for you and good for her. Often, making life easier for yourself also simplifies eating for your child. For example, you will be less upset when your child rejects a sandwich than something you've taken time and trouble to prepare. The less emotion there is involved in her eating, the better she's likely to eat.

It's perfectly possible to have the benefits of breast-feeding without sacrificing the convenience of bottles, and the benefits of home-prepared food without spending time in the kitchen. Home-made food can be fast food. There is no rule that says a good meal needs to be cooked, hot, or made from scratch. Short cuts can make home-made food as fast as opening a jar.

The longer you can keep your child's diet and her eating habits simple and straightforward, the more likely she is to keep it that way herself. The answer is to provide quick, convenient, healthy food at regular intervals and nothing else, except for treats on special occasions.

The simple solution can be summed up in twelve golden rules:

- Allow your baby to eat when she's hungry, but make sure she's hungry before you feed her.
- Let your child stop eating when she's had enough. Feed her less, and let her ask for more.
- Think of it as your job to provide nutritious food, and your child's to eat what she needs. Trust her to regulate her own intake.
- Get breast-feeding well established before introducing a bottle if you want to continue breast-feeding.
- Meet your child's need for attention and emotional satisfaction in non-food ways.

- Allow your baby to feed herself as soon as she shows interest. Introduce finger food as soon as she can manage it.
- Avoid conflict over food. It lays the foundations of eating problems. Remember it takes two to have a battle.
- Plan nutritious snacks as part of your child's diet. This meets her energy needs, prevents the behaviour problems that go with low blood-sugar levels, conserves protein for body-building and avoids cravings for sugar.
- Phase out bottles at the end of your baby's first year. This helps to prevent an emotional attachment to the bottle, a habit of comfort feeding, and overfeeding on milk.
- Keep discipline and eating separate. Behaviour over food and meals is one thing. Eating is another.
- If all the food you offer your child is nutritious, it doesn't much matter what she selects, or how she combines it. Puddings, for example, can consist of fruit and plain yoghurt.
- Treats are for special occasions. If your child has them every day, they're no longer treats.

12

HEALTHY FAST FOOD:
Suggestions, Tips and Recipes

IF THERE is one perfect food, something that sums up the simple solution to feeding babies and small children, it's the banana. Perfectly hygienic, sealed in its own container, a handy size for coat pockets, easily digestible, rich in nutrients and delicious, it makes an ideal weaning food, breakfast, pudding, portable instant snack and supper substitute for tired children.

For parents who care about nutrition, but who are in no hurry to get up and into the kitchen at weekends, a well-timed banana and a cup of milk can buy you a good hour in bed (even if the deal does include stories, cartoons, or making tents out of the duvet), or keep a ravenous nine-month-old happily ignorant of the truth that, as yet, there's no sign of lunch.

Try mashed banana for weaning babies, sliced or whole bananas for finger food, banana and peanut butter sandwiches for toddlers, mashed banana coloured pink for fun. Its only drawback is that it leaves nasty brown stains on white T-shirts.

· KITCHEN HELPERS ·

The two items of equipment that do most to make life with babies and small children easier are a *freezer* and a *microwave*. For a young baby, tiny portions of fruit or vegetable purées, frozen in ice-cube trays, defrost in seconds in a microwave. This means that, once you've made a batch of cubes, there's no need to plan meals in advance. With this method, presenting your baby with a fresh, nutritious, simple, home-made dinner is as easy and quick as opening a jar. Always stir microwaved food as heating can be uneven.

Later, you can cook when you're in the mood, or have the time, or to use up the contents of the fridge, and freeze several portions of casserole or spaghetti sauce in plastic containers. Even if you never use your microwave for anything but defrosting, cooking vegetables and warming food, it's invaluable as a short cut to proper cooking. A portion of cold chicken and rice becomes a hot dinner in one minute, while the fresh vegetables to go with it (cooked in three minutes) are cooling down.

A *blender or food-processor* is useful for making large batches of purée, but not for small quantities, because most will stick to the blades. Many parents prefer to use a *strong metal sieve* and a *wooden spoon*, finding this almost as fast and less messy. Unlike a blender, it also makes sure there are no tough fibres, seeds or lumps in your purée. Another option is a 'mouli'-type grater, which is useful for small quantities.

A *stick-blender*, which can whizz food directly in a saucepan, or in a plastic beaker, to be sealed and go straight into the fridge, is a useful gadget for the purée and finely mashed stage, and can continue to earn its keep for soups, sauces and milk-shakes later on.

• EFFORTLESS WEANING •
THE CUBE SYSTEM

If you can invest half-an-hour's cooking time once a week or so, you can give your baby fresh, tasty, home-cooked food in the time it would take to open a packet.

Baby apple: Peel and core four or five ripe dessert apples and cut into chunks. Cook in a little water until soft. (This takes about five minutes in the microwave, or ten in a saucepan.)

Purée, along with the cooking water, using a blender, or push through a sieve. It will be quite a runny purée, which is easiest for very young babies to suck off the tip of a spoon. Fill a scrupulously clean ice-cube tray with the purée and freeze. When frozen, knock out the cubes into a freezer bag, label and store in the freezer.

One cube is a portion at first. As your baby's eating progresses, he will eat two. Defrost a cube in the microwave for about two minutes, at room temperature for an hour or so, or in the fridge overnight. A cube or two can be transferred to a plastic box when you go out for the day, to defrost until you need it. Serve at room temperature, or lukewarm. If you use a microwave, stir and test the temperature of the purée with a clean finger to make sure that it's not too warm. To suit your baby, you can either make the purée thinner, by adding cooled, boiled water or your baby's usual milk, or thicken it with baby rice.

Baby pear: This can be made in exactly the same way. Or you can freeze a batch of sieved ripe, raw pear.

Baby carrot: Organic carrots are widely available, and taste better than others. Peel and slice about eight carrots. Cook until soft. (About six minutes in the microwave, or fifteen in a saucepan.) Blend or sieve and freeze in an ice-tray as before.

***

Apple, pear and carrot are ideal to have on stand-by. They are easy to purée, with clear, fresh, naturally sweet tastes. When your baby is used to them separately and is hungrier, one of each can be mixed together. They are also good mixers with baby rice, banana, and potato or other vegetables. The cube stage is quite short. When your baby can manage finger food, usually after six months or so, he can pick up small pieces of cooked vegetables, or gnaw on raw vegetables and fruit.

• COOKED FRUIT AND VEGETABLES •

Stewed apple: Apple continues to be extremely useful for older babies and toddlers, for mixing with cereals, or as a pudding, perhaps mixed with Greek yoghurt.

Peel and roughly chop two or three dessert apples (or cooking apples, adding a tablespoon of brown sugar). Add a handful of raisins and a sprinkle of cinnamon if you like. Stew in a little water until soft, about five minutes in a microwave, or ten in a saucepan. Keep in a covered bowl in the fridge for a few days, using as required.

My three-year-old has had this for pudding with Greek yoghurt nearly every day since she was about eight months old.

Baby vegetable casserole: Boil, steam or microwave a mixture of vegetables (for example, carrots, potatoes and leeks) until soft. Blend, sieve or mash with the cooking water. Freeze in small containers, such as cottage-cheese or margarine tubs. Defrost as required. From about nine months, you can ring the changes by adding grated cheese, finely chopped cooked chicken, flaked fish or cooked minced meat before serving.

• FINGER FOODS •

From about six months, your baby will start to sit up, make a grab for the spoon or bits of food on your plate, and be able to chew using his gums. These are signs that he is ready to start feeding himself. Finger food is the ideal method, as it's easier than trying to manage a spoon. *Always stay close by when your baby is eating finger food, to make sure he doesn't choke.*

HOW TO COPE WITH CHOKING

The possibility of choking worries many first-time mothers, especially. This worry may be the reason for continuing to spoon-feed a baby on purées long after he could be enjoying finger food. With some sensible precautions, the risk is small, and certainly no reason to hold your baby back.

Give him small, soft pieces, such as cubes of cooked carrot or potato. Hard food, such as raw apples and carrots, should be big enough for him to hold, mouth and suck. What you want to avoid is small, hard pieces. Keep him well away from nuts, olives, hard sweets, popcorn and slices of sausage and bacon. When he starts having meat, make it minced at first, then chopped up small.

If something does get stuck, don't panic. The gagging reflex is very strong. If you can see the piece of food, hook it out with your finger. If not, hold him upright on your lap and bang his back sharply with the flat of your hand. This makes the piece of food pop out, and he will cry. The crisis is over.

Bread, by itself or as sandwiches, makes perfect finger food. The stage when your baby is ready for finger food happily coincides with the best time to introduce bread into his diet, after six months. *Guidelines on when to introduce other types of food mentioned below can be found in Chapter 9.*

Bread and Sandwiches

Give your baby a crust or slice of bread (white or wholemeal, but preferably not granary) to gnaw on when he's teething, or waiting for a meal. Breadsticks are perfect for the car, the push-chair, and to carry around in a plastic bag or box when you're out and about. They are also good for your baby to dip into mashed fruit or vegetables. This is easier than managing a spoon, more nutritious, and more fun.

Baby open sandwiches: These make appealing and nutritious instant meals. Spread a slice of bread with your chosen filling. Cut off the crusts, then cut twice across and twice down, making nine little squares. Babies love these, and they make fast, fun 'picnics' for toddlers and small children. Arrange over a plate, alternating with bits of fruit or vegetables.

Tea-party sandwiches: These can be a staple item in the diet of babies and small children from about seven months onwards. Make a sandwich, cut off the crusts, then cut into triangles. Babies are intrigued by these, and quickly progress from mouthing them to polishing them off in their entirety.

Fillings: The following are good alone or in combinations:

- Cottage cheese, grated hard, mild cheese, cream cheese, ricotta cheese.
- Mashed banana, avocado pear, apple purée.
- Chopped chicken, chopped liver, tinned tuna, salmon or sardines, taramasalata.
- Hummus (chick pea paste), tahina (sesame seed paste), peanut butter and other nut butters, fruit spreads. These are stocked by many supermarkets as well as health-food shops.
- Yeast extract (very thinly spread), jam, honey.
- Concentrated pure fruit, like a kind of treacle, is available from

health food shops. This is useful for sweetening other food, and as a spread.

Fruit and Vegetables

Cooked vegetables: Cubes of carrot, beetroot, potato, sweet potato, courgette, parsnip. Broccoli and cauliflower florets. Green beans and peas. Quartered Brussels sprouts. Baby corn-on-the-cob.

Raw vegetables: These are especially good for teething babies to gnaw. Whole peeled carrots. Sticks of peeled cucumber or celery.

Fruit: Apple (whole or peeled and quartered), pear (whole or peeled and quartered), banana (whole or sliced), avocado pear (cubed), cherries (stoned and halved), tangerines (seedless segments), seedless grapes, mango, melon and papaya (peeled and sliced, seeds removed), peaches, apricots, plums (stoned, peeled and sliced), strawberries, raspberries. Quartered cherry tomatoes.

Other Finger Foods

Cereals: Dry cereal is fun for babies to pick up in their fingers. It's also handy to carry in a small plastic bag when out and about. Examples of suitable unsweetened cereals are cornflakes, puffed rice, bite-sized shredded wheat (this also comes with fruit fillings), and granola.

Pasta: Chopped spaghetti, or small pasta shapes.

Meat, chicken and fish: Small pieces of cooked chicken or turkey. Strips of cooked liver. Fish-fingers. Bits of fish-cakes. Small pieces of cooked white fish. Flakes of tinned tuna or salmon. Chopped hard-boiled eggs. Meatballs.

• FAST FISH •

White fish, in particular, is light, digestible and nutritious, making it excellent for babies. Fish-fingers are fast, and popular with most children from nine months or so.

Another good freezer stand-by is individual boil-in-the-bag portions of fish, such as 'cod in butter sauce'. These take fifteen minutes to cook. They make an excellent dinner for an older baby or toddler, enough for two meals. (The unused portion can be kept in a sealed plastic box in the fridge for twenty-four hours.)

Once cooked, the fish and sauce can be mashed into vegetables for babies, or served on half a microwaved baked potato, along with some frozen peas or other vegetables as a sort of fast fish pie for toddlers.

Oily fish, such as tuna and sardines, is more difficult to digest and should be introduced later than white fish. Sardines on toast and tuna sandwiches both make high-protein, well-balanced, fast-food meals.

• EVERYDAY FOOD FOR YOUR BABY •

Most of the food we eat is suitable for older babies. Cook more than you need at supper-time and give what's left to your baby the next day.

Rice: Cooked rice (brown or white) can be mixed with mashed vegetables, served as finger food with meat or fish and vegetables, or mixed with yoghurt and fruit for a rice pudding.

Cold meat: A cold roast chicken (or other roast joint of meat) is a useful thing to have in the fridge. If you cook an extra-large roast on Sunday, you can heat individual portions of the cold meat and gravy in the microwave to serve with already cooked rice and freshly microwaved vegetables for toddler lunch for the next day or two. This sort of plain, tasty food goes down well, and the meal takes a total of five minutes to produce.

Pasta: Pasta is usually popular with babies and children. Your baby can have some of yours mashed up, as long as the sauce ingredients are suitable. Avoid chilli generally, and bacon and tomato-based sauces for a baby under nine months or so; give him butter and/or grated cheese on his portion instead. Creamy, garlicky sauces are fine. If you cook pasta especially for him, use small shapes, or chopped-up spaghetti, and mix with grated cheese or butter. Add chopped or puréed vegetables, or puréed tomato for older babies. Miniature pasta shapes take three minutes to cook. If you use these and ready-made sieved tomato (available in jars and cartons, and called passata), this makes a five-minute main meal that most babies and children seem to love.

Yoghurt: Full-cream, Greek-style, plain yoghurt is the most versatile and nutritious one to buy. It can be mixed with stewed fruit or mashed banana for puddings, with fruit and cereal for breakfast, with cooked rice and chopped vegetables for instant risotto, or used in cooking. Fruit-flavoured yoghurts marketed for babies and toddlers are a bad buy, as they're full of sugar and expensive.

Cheese: Many babies enjoy gnawing on a chunk of mild cheese. Ricotta cheese (a full-fat curd cheese sold in tubs) and *fromage frais* are both delicious with fruit, as well as pasta and vegetables. Cheese and pulses, such as baked beans, go well together and make nutritious, high-protein vegetarian meals, especially with bread. Soup made with dried pulses (beans, peas or lentils) can be served with grated cheese and a hunk of bread, or a cheese sandwich. Grated cheese sprinkled over baked beans on toast is a good fast dinner for older babies and toddlers.

Liver: The Simple Solution

Liver is highly nutritious, an especially rich source of iron as well as protein. Unfortunately, adults who don't like liver themselves tend not to give it to their children. In addition, the tastiest and tenderest liver, calves' liver, is expensive, and needs to be cooked while very fresh.

There is a simple solution to hand. Frozen chicken livers, sold in tubs, have a mild, sweet flavour that many toddlers love. Because they're frozen, you can keep them in your freezer until you want to cook them. They're quick to cook, and one of the cheapest sources of first-class protein you can buy.

Chicken livers in tomato sauce
1 tub frozen chicken livers, defrosted
1 onion, finely chopped

2 rashers bacon, chopped (optional)
2 cloves garlic, crushed
1 tin chopped tomatoes
1 teaspoon sugar
2 tablespoons olive or sunflower oil

Heat the oil in a shallow pan. Add the chopped bacon, if using. Add the onion and garlic and cook until translucent. Add the chicken livers. Cook until stiffened and browned. Add the tomatoes and their juice, together with the sugar, which helps to bring out the tomato flavour. Bring to the boil and simmer for about half an hour, until the tomatoes have thickened.

Serve with rice, baked or mashed potato, or on toast. This makes enough for one or two adults and a child, depending on appetite, or four children. Extra portions can be frozen.

For a change, add a thinly sliced carrot together with the onion, or add frozen peas or sliced fresh mushrooms for the last five minutes of cooking.

Home-made chicken-liver pâté
1 tub frozen chicken livers, defrosted
1 onion, finely chopped
2 cloves garlic, crushed
2 tablespoons olive or sunflower oil
2 tablespoons butter

Heat the butter and oil together and cook the onion and garlic until translucent. Add the chicken livers and cook until stiffened and brown. Cut one in half to check that they are cooked through. The livers will take about fifteen minutes to cook.

Whizz in a blender or mash with a fork. This is good on sandwiches, crackers or squares of toast. It can be kept in the fridge for several days in a sealed container.

• WHAT TO BUY INSTEAD OF • BABY FOOD

There is no need to buy any food specially prepared for babies, except perhaps baby rice for the first weeks of solids. However,

139

there are plenty of ready-to-eat and convenience foods on the super-market shelves which are worth buying, as they help you produce fast, healthy meals without fuss.

Here is a basic shopping list, including the fresh and ready-made items mentioned above, as well as healthy snacks and treats.

Fresh food
Fruit, fresh and dried
Vegetables
Chicken, fresh, and free range if possible
Meat, organic if possible
Eggs, free range if possible

Frozen food
Frozen chicken livers
Frozen fish-fingers
Frozen boil-in-the-bag portions of cod in butter sauce
Frozen peas and other vegetables

Tins and cartons
Tinned tomatoes
Tinned baked beans (low-sugar variety if possible)
Tinned tuna, salmon and sardines
Cartons of sieved tomatoes (passata)

Dairy products
Greek yoghurt
Cottage cheese, cream cheese, ricotta cheese or *fromage frais*
Mild hard cheese, such as Edam, Gouda or mild Cheddar

Delicatessen
Hummus
Taramasalata

Cereals
Porridge oats, or instant oatmeal
Weetabix™, shredded wheat, muesli, granola
Bread (extra for the freezer)

Portable snacks
Bananas, apples, pears, tangerines
Bread sticks, oatcakes, rice-cakes, crispbreads
Cereals, such as granola, or fruit-filled, bite-sized
shredded wheat
Dried fruit, especially raisins in little boxes (these are high in
sugar, but toddlers love them, and they make good treats)

FEEDING PLAN FOR FAST FOOD WITHOUT FUSS

▶ A freezer and a microwave will be your most valuable allies.
They allow you to produce a hot, fresh meal in minutes, and to
make full use of healthy convenience foods.
▶ The cube system of freezing fresh fruit and vegetable purées
allows you to feed a young baby an ideal diet while spending
almost no time cooking.
▶ When you cook, make more than you need. Freeze extra portions
in small containers, or base meals on what's left over.
▶ Cooked apple and cooked rice are useful to have in the fridge.
▶ Bread and sandwiches can become an increasingly important part
of your child's diet from about six months onwards.
▶ Frozen chicken livers are a convenient, easy, cheap, tasty way to
give babies and children the nutritional benefits of liver.
▶ There's no need to buy anything especially made for babies. Baby
yoghurts and baby rusks, for example, are high in sugar and
expensive. However, many ready-to-eat and convenience foods
are a great help in producing fast, healthy food without fuss.
▶ If there's one perfect, instant, portable, hygienic and delicious
food, suitable from weaning onwards, it's the banana.

INDEX

overeating, during pregnancy, 26–7, 30
overfeeding, 11–12
  baby food and, 81
  bottle-feeding, 91
  fat babies, 126–7
  milk and, 11, 12
  protein, 105
  sugar and, 109

pasta, 136, 137–8
pâté, chicken-liver, 139
peanut allergy, 107– 8, 112
peanut butter, 96, 108, 112
pears, puréed, 133
porridge, 96
portion size, 117
power
  emotional associations of food, 24
  faddy eaters, 126
pregnancy, 21–2, 26–7, 29–31
protein, 17, 18, 81, 90, 96, 105, 107, 112
puddings, 95, 102, 125
pumps, expressing breast milk, 52
punishment, emotional associations of food, 24–5
purées, frozen, 92–3, 131–3

reflex, 'rooting', 50
restless babies, settling, 49–50
rewards, food as, 24–5
rice, 71–2, 86, 137
'rooting reflex', 50
refusing to eat, 115–18, 123–4
rusks, 94

salmonella, 112
salt, 110
sandwiches, 94, 134, 135–6
schedule feeding, 16, 60–1, 62–4, 66–7
self-feeding, 120
  see also finger food
self-image, 25
settling restless babies, 49–50
sieves, 132
snacks, 17, 89–90, 92, 103–4, 141
social skills, 79
solids
  baby food, 78–88
  and baby's development, 80
  cube system, 92–3, 132–3
  and drinking water, 100–1
  eating patterns, 97–100
  introducing, 16–17, 68–73, 74–7, 92–3
  introducing new foods, 72, 110–14

and milk, 90–1
  overfeeding, 11–12
  snacks, 89–90, 92, 103–4
soya protein, 107
spoon-feeding, 71, 72, 79, 86, 93, 118, 120
starches, in baby food, 17, 81, 83
sterilizing equipment, 57, 71
stick-blenders, 132
sucking
  breast-feeding, 43, 44, 45, 48
  'comfort-sucking', 65
  dummies, 50
sugar, 109
  in baby food, 17, 81, 83
  blood-sugar levels, 12, 90, 109, 124
  in drinks, 101
supper, 96
swaddling, 49
sweet tooth, 81, 102
sweets, 102–3

tantrums, 124–5
tea (drink), 102
tea (meal), 96
teats, bottle-feeding, 56, 57
teething, 94–5
texture, baby food, 85
'time-out' approach, 125
tinned food, 140
toast, 94, 95
tomatoes, 72, 84, 96, 112
tooth decay, 102, 109
top-up bottles, 45, 47, 54
treats, 102–4, 116, 125

underfeeding, 11, 12, 109

vegetables
  in baby food, 85, 87
  baby vegetable casserole, 133–4
  finger foods, 136
  frozen purées, 92–3, 131–2
  introducing solids, 72, 80, 85–6
  likes and dislikes, 23
vegetarian diet, 96
vitamins, 27, 101

water, drinking, 74, 100–1
weaning, 54, 55, 75-7, 132–3
weight, birth weight, 28–9
weight gain
  baby's, 13
  during pregnancy, 27
wheat, 18, 94

yoghurt, 95, 107, 138